Set Margins' #52
Conspiratorial Design
Information Design for the Bigger Picture
by Carlo Bramanti

ISBN: 978-90-834498-7-6

Graphic design: Carlo Bramanti, Sofia Paz
Advisor: Silvio Lorusso, Freek Lomme, James Dyer
Text editor: James Dyer
Printer: AS Printon
Typeset in: Adobe Jenson, Menco
First edition: 2025

On the front cover:
Richard Buckminster Fuller holding a geodesic tensegrity sphere.

The citations from Italian were translated by the author.

Every effort has been made to contact copyright holders and to obtain their permission for the use of copyright material. If inadvertent infringement has occurred please contact the publisher.

This publication is licensed under a Creative Commons Attribution-NonCommercial-ShareAlike 4.0 International Licence (CC BY-NC-SA 4.0). To view a copy of this license, visit: https://creativecommons.org/licenses/by-nc-sa/4.0/

Set Margins'
www.setmargins.press

CONSPIRATORIAL DESIGN
**INFORMATION DESIGN
FOR THE BIGGER PICTURE**

CARLO BRAMANTI

SET MARGINS' #52

CONSPIRATORIAL DESIGN
INFORMATION DESIGN FOR THE BIGGER PICTURE

We suspect something terrible to be going on behind the design—cynical manipulation, political propaganda, hidden intrigues, vested interests, crimes. Following the death of God, the conspiracy theory became the only surviving form of traditional metaphysics as a discourse about the hidden and the invisible. Where we once had nature and God, we now have design and conspiracy theory.

Boris Groys

TABLE OF CONTENTS

INTRODUCTION 10

CONNECTING THE DOTS: 16
FIRST SUSPICIONS
    Premise 17
    Contemporary Conspiracy Theories 20
    Information Design 26

DRAWING THE BORDERS: 54
US AND THEM
    How to Draw a Line 55
    Dark Pessimism 59
    Breathing Together 67

LOOKING FOR PATTERNS: 88
CONSPIRATORIAL DESIGN
    Styles and Roles 89
    A Taxonomy 97
    Esoteric Traditions 102

SEEING IT ALL: 138
THE BIGGER PICTURE
    Confirmations Only 139
    The Bigger Picture 142

CONCLUSION 162

AFTERWORD "AGAINST COMPLEXITY" 172
BY SILVIO LORUSSO

ACKNOWLEDGEMENTS 180

BIBLIOGRAPHY 182

INTRODUCTION

This book deals with design and conspiracy theories, two things that are often thought of as opposites. Design is generally perceived as something that simplifies and targets the essence of things; something that should say the Truth. Conspiracy theories instead are far-fetched and unwieldy, they create confusion: exactly what a designer should dispel easily. Design is expected to be able to bypass misinformation and false rhetorics because its very premise is to deal with how things work *in reality*. However, what I argue in this book is that design, especially information design, and conspiracy theories mirror each other. They act with similar goals and they adopt comparable representations. They intersect in their practices and in their artifacts because they share a common ground at their fundaments. I call this common ground *Conspiratorial Design*.

I must admit that I find a twisted beauty in the world of conspiracy theories. I am captivated by their peculiar narrative structures, their frequent allusions to ancient esoteric symbolism, and the way the same core stories recur throughout history. This research started in 2022 while doing my MA in Information Design at Design Academy Eindhoven when I stumbled across a particularly inspiring diagram: the *Q-WEB*. The Q-WEB is a hyper-dense, labyrinthine, but meticulously crafted conspiracy diagram that became extremely successful among the followers of contemporary American conspiracy theories. Seeing it put me in front of a distorted mirror: someone was approaching my discipline—information design—in a completely different way, more obscure, more obsessed. In trying to understand conspiracy theories I found myself sympathizing with the deep-seated human need to impose meaning on an often inscrutable and cruel reality. At the same time, I recognized the narrative strength of such a phenomenon, that transforms existential uncertainty into a game: for many, connecting the dots—even when those dots form a disturbing picture—is an adventure in itself. That said, my fascination for conspiracy theories is not the central focus of this text. What I want to do is critically examine whether a true analytical distance from conspiracy theories is possible, particularly from my own position as an information designer.

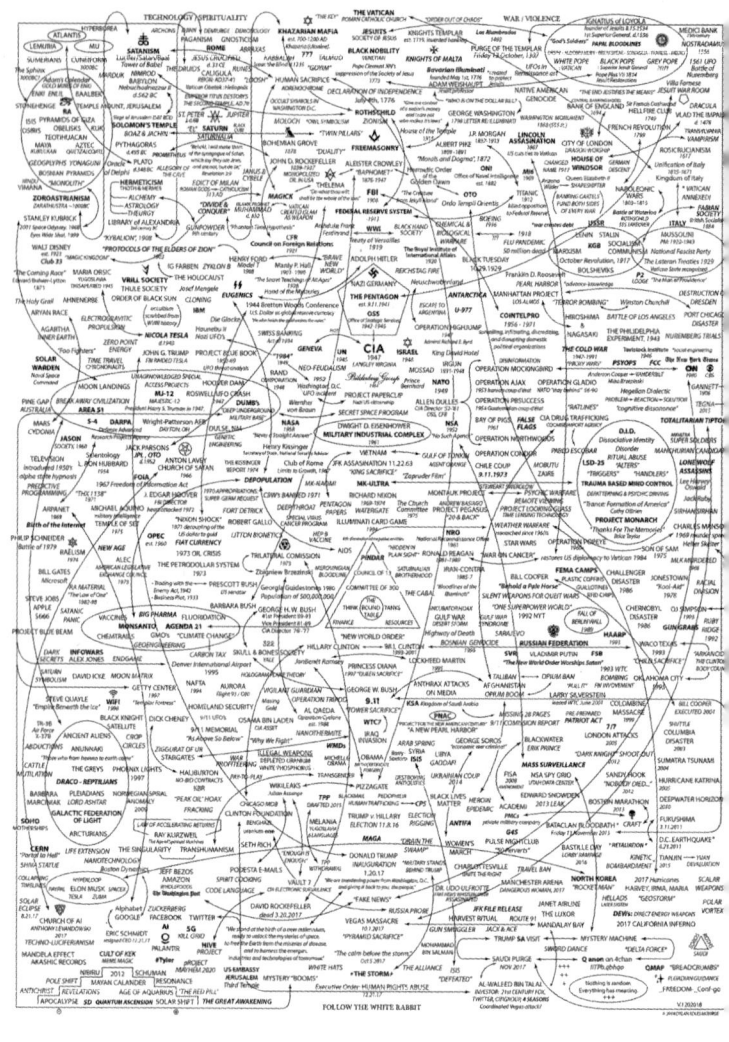

fig. 1   Q-WEB, Dylan Louis Monroe, 2018.
Digital. 8.5 x 11 in. www.deepstatemappingproject.com

Detail from fig. 1

> Nothing is random.
> Everything has meaning.
> +++

Detail from fig. 1

PART I.
CONNECTING THE DOTS: FIRST SUSPICIONS

A. PREMISE
B. CONTEMPORARY CONSPIRACY THEORIES
C. INFORMATION DESIGN

A.
PREMISE

Before delving into the arguments of this publication, I want to describe some of the challenges it has presented to me. Writing about design and conspiracy theories is, in a sense, a dual attempt—both to observe myself and to gain an aerial view of the intricate maze I find myself navigating. On the one hand, this work requires a self-critical analysis of the professional field to which I belong: design. On the other hand, engaging with conspiracy theories has made me realize that they are not something that I can examine from a detached perspective. Instead, I must acknowledge that I, too, am implicated in the mindset they reflect. I strongly resonate with the struggles articulated by writer Gregorio Magini in *Mitologia del Complottismo*,[1] where he poses a question analogous to the one that moves me: "What do I share with a conspiracy theorist?" He adopts what he calls a "comprehensive approach to conspiracy theories," which does not dismiss them as a pathological condition affecting only certain individuals. Rather, he considers the conspiratorial mindset a normal but harmful habit of rationality—something that cannot be fully distanced from, even by those who believe themselves immune. Attempting to recognize the conspiracy theorist within oneself, however, presents an analytical paradox. As Magini puts it, "One cannot simultaneously dive into the abyss and observe the landscape from above."

---

1   Gregorio Magini, *Mitologia del complottismo: il Behemoth delle storie*, 2024.

In other words, one must choose from what point of view to observe the maze: from a pedestal or immersed in the abyss, each having its own quality. Nonetheless, I think adopting a comprehensive approach (staying in the abyss) does not necessarily imply indifference or neutrality. The kind of perspective I wish to adopt in this sense is similar to the one taken by Richard Hofstadter, who, in *The Paranoid Style in American Politics*, introduces the concept of the paranoid style as a way of understanding conspiracy theories while maintaining a critical stance.

> When I speak of the paranoid style, I use the term much as an art historian might speak of the baroque or the mannerist style. It is, above all, a way of seeing the world and of expressing oneself. [...] Of course, the term 'paranoid style' is pejorative, and it is meant to be; the paranoid style has a greater affinity for bad causes than good. But nothing entirely prevents a sound program or a sound issue from being advocated in the paranoid style, and it is admittedly impossible to settle the merits of an argument because we think we hear in its presentation the characteristic paranoid accents. Style has to do with the way in which ideas are believed and advocated rather than with the truth or falsity of their content.[2]

---

2   Richard Hofstadter, *The Paranoid Style in American Politics, and Other Essays*, 1964.

The second challenge of this text is ensuring that this comparison is both balanced and meaningful. Are conspiracy theories merely a pretext for me to discuss design? Or is it the other way around? What insights can such a comparison offer, and what vision of the world does it imply? On one side, there is the risk of being misinterpreted as sympathetic to neo-fascist conspiracy theories supporters; on the other, of being perceived as anti-intellectual for critiquing critique itself. I do not mean to be either. I reject fascist ideologies, which I see as oppressive distortions of history and reality. At the same time, I am not an anti-intellectual as my intent is not to dismiss intellectual critique but rather to examine its limitations—particularly in the context of design discourse, where self-reflection sometimes risks becoming self-indulgence. Perhaps, rather than a direct comparison, *Conspiratorial Design* is an attempt to document a liminal landscape—its intersections, its origins, and the ways in which it manifests itself. While my perspective on this landscape is necessarily limited, this publication also aims to serve as a work-in-progress guide on the topic of design and conspiracy theories, offering references to key authors and case studies alongside my own reflections.

One final premise I find necessary is acknowledging the gravity of the topic. Analyzing conspiracy theories means confronting ideas and events that are far from harmless—many are deeply entangled with some of humanity's worst instincts. The desire for absolute explanations, free from uncertainty, has often been used as a pretext for discrimination and violence. The examples are sadly numerous: anti-semitic conspiracy theories were used to incentivize racial laws in Italy during fascism; the "Great Replacement" theory, which falsely claims that elites are orchestrating the demographic replacement of white populations, has fueled many cases of extremist violence, including the Christchurch mosque shootings in 2019; and the infamous Comet Ping Pong episode in 2016, that originated from the Pizzagate conspiracy theory, was just the first manifestation of the deep net of contemporary American far right conspiracy theories. While I fully recognize the dangers of this kind of belief, my approach here is to momentarily suspend judgment to reflect on the underlying mechanisms of conspiratorial thinking. Maintaining this analytical distance is, of course, very difficult. However, if one manages—if only for a moment—to put oneself in the paranoid shoes, certain fascinating aspects of this unrestrained imaginative process begin to emerge.

B.

CONTEMPORARY CONSPIRACY THEORIES

Conspiracy theories seem to have become an indelible part of the discussion about mass information. Whenever an event gets extensive media coverage—either for its dramatic nature, international relevance, or simply just its oddity—it's almost certain that someone somewhere online will come up with an alternative interpretation of the known facts and propose a backstory. Watching a political debate on

TV where someone with absurd beliefs is acting as a lunatic that agitates the discussion is something most people have probably experienced. Commenting on the most unreasonable theories has become for many a mundane activity, to the point where making a joke on, for example, flat-earthers is an easygoing way to show your belonging to the rational part of humanity: *Can you believe people out there are believing this crazy stuff? Not us though, we are sane.*

While I participated in this process of normalization, I recently started to ask myself: How did this start? I don't have the space (and probably neither the knowledge) to make an exhaustive history of conspiracy theories. Still, looking at historical examples of conspiracy theories can bring up how certain social cognitive behaviors related to fear have been around basically for all of human history, and how they have often been instrumentalized for political reasons. A classic example that stands out in the 20th century are the conspiracy theories revolving around *The Protocols of Elders of Zion*. In that case, a fake document was produced at the beginning of the 20th century to testify about an alleged Jewish conspiracy against Russia, in order to foment racial hate and consolidate governmental power. The protocols are also a notable case study for the notion of post-truth since even after they were recognized as false (very soon after their production), they kept on having the desired effect in terms of political narrative. As I said, conspiracy theories are a phenomenon with a long history. In this text though I will mainly deal with more contemporary conspiracy theories because, in my opinion, the dynamics of propagation in the communities and the way they interact with media and information technologies make them a phenomenon worth analyzing separately.

One useful set of coordinates that was very useful to start understanding and navigating the vast panorama of contemporary conspiracy theories is the taxonomy proposed by Michael Barkun in *A Culture of Conspiracy*[3] which divides conspiracy theories into "event conspiracies", "systemic conspiracies", and "super conspiracies". Event conspiracies are the ones revolving around one single event, like for example the ones about the assassination of JFK. Systemic conspiracies are about exposing one single source of evil that operates various interconnected plots. Super conspiracies are hatched by multiple secret groups to govern all systems over an extremely long time period.

If these categories were useful to navigate conspiracy theories in the early 2000s, I think an important step forward was made by Wu Ming 1 In *La di Q di Qomplotto*.[4] There, he clarifies the important distinction between the hypothesis of an actual conspiracy, (which are rare but existing events) from a conspiracy theory or "conspiracy fantasy." The main difference between the hypothesis of an actual conspiracy (that is, a secret deal between a set number of participants with the malevolent purpose of harming

---

[3] Michael Barkun, *A Culture of Conspiracy: Apocalyptic Visions in Contemporary America*, 2006.
[4] Wu Ming 1, *La Q Di Qomplotto: QAnon e Dintorni: Come Le Fantasie Di Complotto Difendono Il Sistema*, 2021.

someone else) and a conspiracy fantasy is basically *indefiniteness*. Wu Ming 1's conception of conspiracy theory is quite similar to the one of Barkun's "super conspiracy", but it extends even further. To him, the true essence of contemporary conspiracy theories is a fantasy of a plan with extreme ambitions (eventually world dominance, usually), carried out by an indefinite, and usually increasing, set of actors, during an indefinite time period. In this conception of conspiracy theories, indefiniteness plays a central role, as it allows for a constant mutability of the theory that makes it a perfectly elastic framework. This allows everybody to encompass single events into a larger understanding. Through this constant mutation conspiracy theories become impossible to unveil and therefore any attempt to debunk them becomes useless, if not even pointless.

A big part of the common imagery of conspiracy theories comes from the 1990s and early 2000s when they started to become a popular cultural phenomenon. Inspired and probably feeling seen by pop culture works dealing with mysteries, like *The X Files*, people with all sorts of fascinations for underground countercultures, esoterism, and skeptical towards mainstream information, found in online forums a fertile environment to cultivate and share their visions of the world. With the birth of online imageboards in the early 2000s these environments thrived. Imageboards are a type of Internet forum that focuses on the posting of images, some of which also allow for anonymity. The most notable example is 4chan, which was a fundamental node in the development of the knotty social dynamic where contemporary conspiracy theories were incubated. In particular, 4chan was the place where the most influential conspiracy theory in recent history developed: QAnon. QAnon is a far-right conspiracy theory mainly widespread in the United States that proposes the existence of a secret cabal of satanic ritual abusers that dominates the world through politics and mediatic control. QAnon followers also believe that Donald Trump is the leader of the opposition in a secret war against this evil cabal. A widespread belief is that the members of the cannibalistic cabal—of which some prominent members are Hilary Clinton, George Soros, and Tom Hanks—are abusing children to harvest adrenochrome (a chemical compound) by extracting it from their eyes to then use it as an Elixir of life. But not every follower of QAnon is equally concerned with the occultist aspects. Some are dealing more with theories about the American Deep State that don't have any supernatural aspect. The presence of variations in the theory is due to the fact that, like almost every other conspiracy theory, the core of the belief is not univocal, it embraces countless hypotheses of hidden truths and it's in constant re-elaboration by its community. The years from 2016 to 2020 were a key moment for the diffusion of conspiracy theories. The conjunction between the relationship of Trump administration with QAnon and the emergence of COVID-19, as well as all the other factors of the political and economic instability of those years, forced everybody to face a newly esoteric approach to information that for a moment seemed to have become majoritarian. That wave of conspiracy theories had a symbolic culmination with the attack on Capitol Hill in January 2021. After that, the diffusion of QAnon, as well as many other conspiracy theories, seemed to have partially downsized. There could have been various causes for this. The attack on Capitol Hill exposed QAnon to the world as a cult of violent delusional fanatics. The end of the pandemic slowly brought everybody back to a sense of normality. Some social media platforms started implementing more stringent policies in their algorithms to try to limit fake news. Today, with the re-election of Donald Trump, all of this seems to be starting again and many are preparing to face another wave of absurdity. Anti-vaccine activist Robert F. Kennedy Jr. was nominated for United States Secretary of Health in Trump's cabinet. Mark Zuckerberg announced that Meta will step back with fact-checking on their platforms.

The relevance of a discussion around conspiracy theories remains unchanged as every new moment of instability reminds us how easy it is for conspiratorial approaches to take hold in our information environment. Conspiracy theories are not something we will get rid of soon and trying to understand how they work will be more and more necessary. I'm not sure it will be enough to stop the phenomenon, but it allows us to open important discussions on our knowledge systems and on what to do with conspiratorial minds, starting with our own.

C.
INFORMATION DESIGN

The other object of study of this text—design—is a field that constantly tries to escape from any attempt to be clearly defined, and even simply noticing this can bring up some interesting reflections. One could say that design is a discipline that consists of finding innovative solutions to problems or fulfilling needs while applying its methods to different fields. This would be already a vast enough definition, also considering that the amount of fields where the methods of design are applied is in constant expansion. However, even this definition would raise objections, as it excludes the opposing anti-consumeristic idea of design as a critical intervention. We could then speak broadly about design as the capacity to prefigure, to imagine a structure before it is built.[5] The issue with such generic definitions though, is that the broader they are, the less useful they become. Silvio Lorusso documents the expanded conception of design, according to which everyone is a designer and everything is design, in a timeline of what he defines as *Design Panism*.[6] Lorusso points out that this vision of design is not just a definitional struggle but also "a rhetorical instrument and a semi-conscious expansion agenda". I point this out because when relating it with conspiracy theories I think it is interesting to notice how many designers want to not just deal with everything, but also with

5   Silvio Lorusso, *What Design Can't Do: Essays on Design and Disillusion*, 2023, p 85.
6   Silvio Lorusso, *Design Panism: A Timeline*, Institute of Network Cultures, March 28, 2021.

everythingness. Meaning that they want to deal with every component of a system and at the same time with the system in its entirety. Advocating for such vastness in the definition of design is in my opinion a stratagem to maintain the idea of the designer as an essential figure: the mastermind who has just enough knowledge of everything to surveil over everyone else's work (an all-seeing eye, to put it in conspiratorial terms). For the purpose of this text, it's not necessary to arrive at a conclusive definition of design but I find it interesting to notice how design shares with conspiracy theories this tension towards an indefinite metadisciplinarity.

To get a bit more specific let's look more closely at the field of design I mainly deal with in this text: information design. Also in this restricted field there are some overlaps in definitions among adjacent fields, like information design, communication design, graphic design, visual design, and the like. A definition of information design that is currently present on Wikipedia is "explanation design",[7] which I find simple yet quite clear. Basically we are speaking of the work of those who elaborate artifacts (mainly visual) to explain something. What's easy to extract from this simple definition, is that there is an underlying pedagogical purpose in the field: there are people to educate and designers who can select and elaborate the data for them, sometimes with the help of scientists and journalists, to provide them with a truthful narrative. In this regard, it is important to remember that data alone

[7] *Information Design*, Wikipedia Foundation. Last edited on 16 March 2025, at 11:18 (UTC).

are not facts but potential arguments, and data visualizations are clarifications of those arguments. As Johanna Drucker explains in *Graphesis: Visual Forms of Knowledge Production*:

> Most information visualizations are acts of interpretation masquerading as presentation. In other words, they are images that act as if they are just showing us what is, but in actuality, they are arguments made in graphical form. But paradoxically, the primary effect of visual forms of knowledge production in any medium [...] is to mask the very fact of their visuality, to render invisible the very means through which they function as argument.[8]

Even though the term "information design" didn't take hold before the 1950s, the idea to adopt a rational and quantified approach to visual communication has many precedents, but we could simplify and identify the 20th century as the moment in which ideals of modernity stimulated more strongly the rise of self-conscious information design practices, also through influential figures like Otto Neurath and more recently Edward Tufte. An interesting case from the history of information design is the book *Graphic Presentation* by Willard C. Brinton, a pioneering information design manual from 1914. The preface, written by Henry Hubbard, opens with a striking passage that imbues graphs with an almost mystical power:

---

8   Johanna Drucker, *Graphesis: Visual Forms of Knowledge Production*, 2014.

CONSPIRATORIAL DESIGN

> There is a magic in graphs. The profile of a curve reveals in a flash a whole situation—the life history of an epidemic, a panic, or an era of prosperity. The curve informs the mind, awakens the imagination, convinces.[9]

Although clearly metaphorical and emphatic, I find this statement a testament to a tension between a modern, positivist view of graphs as objective tools of analysis and an older, almost premodern perception of diagrammatic forms as magic vessels of revelation. While today we think of graphs as rational instruments, Hubbard's language suggests something more intuitive—an almost divine ability to synthesize truth and illuminate the mind.

Today, we have forms of information design (as well as many other fields of design) that have been partially detached from their commercial purpose, even if mainly in the restricted contexts that privilege a more cultural mission. Various designers, like the Italian Radical Design in the 1960s, contributed to shaping the idea that the purpose of design could also be to provoke the audience and raise awareness about social issues. For this reason nowadays when we speak of information design we don't mean just a technical illustration for a car manual or a data visualization in a school book, but also politically engaged artworks exhibited in museums. These were the kinds of works I was prompted to engage with during my design education, to understand how information design could be used to raise awareness on

---

9   Willard Cope Brinton, *Graphic Presentation*, 1939.

matters of politics, technology, justice, and pretty much everything that students and professionals are able to put forward as urgent. In this context, I encountered many works that embody what Patricio Davilla called *Diagrams of Power*[10]: diagrammatic visualizations of power structures and other issues of public relevance that would otherwise be invisible. To make some examples, I'm thinking of works of political information designers in the strict sense like Giorgia Lupi, Stefanie Posavec, Federica Fragapane but also more broadly of artists, researchers, and unconventional practitioners like Metahaven, Trevor Paglen, Paolo Cirio, Heath Bunting, Mark Lombardi, Kate Crawford and Vladan Joler. At the same time while researching conspiracy theories for my MA thesis, I started noticing how conspiracy environments on different online platforms were teeming with artifacts that we can recognize, in every respect, as information design: data visualizations, maps, infographics, and most importantly, diagrams. The themes of these materials were usually the typical conspiratorial obsessions: from putting together the visual evidence of 9/11 as an inside job to flowcharting how mass mind control is corrupting society by pushing it to abandon traditional christian values. A hypothesis could be that this phenomenon started in the early 2000s when many conspiracy theories were still long-form texts on wacky online forums. It was only with the diffusion of imageboards, that the propagation of conspiracy content became less text-centered and more image-centered. Until

10 Patricio Dávila, *Diagrams of Power: Visualizing, Mapping, and Performing Resistance*, 2023.

that moment the diffusion of conspiracy theories still happened through impenetrable walls of text densely packed with intricate interconnected information: a kind of content that was perfect to be transmitted with more synthetic visual means. Besides that, using diagrams usually brings a sense of logic, cohesion, and consequentiality to the content, helping to make it overall more persuasive. This use of the visual language of design can be interpreted as an attempt to gain legitimacy by appropriating the means of a field that has a reputation for working for the good and advancement of society through rationality and innovation (although, to be fair, in the collective conception complex diagrams probably belong more to the domain of science than design).

Observing this, triggered my desire to put conspiracy theories and design side by side, to analyze the rhetorics of their means, and to put this in relation to what I was seeing happening around me in the world of design. I started noticing how many design projects shared with conspiracy theories what I mentioned earlier as a tendency towards indefiniteness as well as thinking in terms of large-scale systems. Many designers base their practice on a programmatic "hyperconnectivity",[11] bridging every possible discipline, field of knowledge, and skill to create a larger understanding of the world as a unitary system. What I propose is that we could think of design and conspiracy theories as two visions of the world that have informed each other. Even though they stem from distant social con-

---

11 Concept used by Silvio Lorusso in *What Design Can't Do: Essays on Design and Disillusion*, 2023. p 98

texts, they have a fundamental drive in common that makes them meet. This unusual mixture produces, rather than a practice, a style, in a sense, the manifestation of Hostadter's paranoid style into design. Let's call it *conspiratorial design*. The point I will try to make is not that design and conspiracy theories are the same thing, but rather that they are two expressions of similar core ideas. Clearly there are also major differences between the two. For example, design is a discipline that is for the most part output-driven, in the sense that designers usually employ theory in their work, but only as a tool, with the final goal to produce some sort of artifact that is supposed to make the world a better place. Conspiracy theories don't have that ambition as they are more research-driven. In the sense that the only way they aim at making a change is by figuring out what are the forces moving events, and in this effort the production of artifacts is collateral. Nonetheless, I think adopting the lens of conspiratorial design can be stimulating and bring up the discomforting point made by Robert Pietrusko in his lecture *Dark Optimism: Conspiratorial Styles of Reasoning for the Biosphere* where he states:

> On closer inspection, it is difficult to locate a methodological distinction between the conspiracy theories we find delusional, dangerous or worse and the techniques of critical inquiry that reveal real systems of power and exploitation.[12]

12 Robert Pietrusko, *Dark Optimism: Conspiratorial Styles of Reasoning for the Biosphere*, Transmediale, February 2022.

CONSPIRATORIAL DESIGN

For this reason in this text, there will be moments in which I will use the term "conspiratorial design" to address both design* and conspiracy theories. With this juxtaposition I have no interest in being judgemental: neither in elevating conspiracy theories nor addressing designers as irrational fools. My intention is rather to show how these two activities try to respond to the same human desire for meaning and order.

Based on what I put on the table I think it can be interesting to sketch a definition of conspiratorial design: *A disposition towards information that uses design methods and tools of representation to achieve a hypertrophic synthesis. The conspiratorial designer assumes that there is a hidden and emergent knowledge they can disclose because they have a privileged total perspective to see the bigger picture. Through conspiratorial design one can see and make others see the invisible connections between the dots that form the greater whole.* I will later get into more detail about the idea of "hypertrophic synthesis", but before that, I think it's necessary to explore the issue of *who* is conspiratorial.

---

* This text contains examples both from the world of art and design without a clear distinction. Placing the line between art and design is complicated and it's not the purpose of this text but at the same time, I don't mean to use this blurriness to my advantage. For the sake of simplicity, the discipline I refer to is the one—however one wants to define it—taught in art and design schools.

CONNECTING THE DOTS

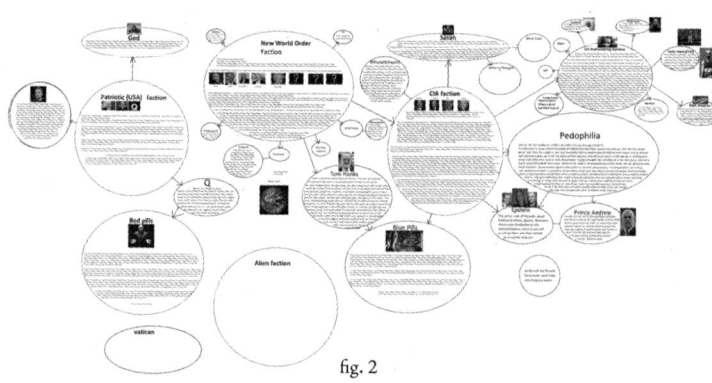

fig. 2

fig. 3

fig. 2 to fig. 9   Unknown authors, results for the query "diagram" in the subreddit r/conspiracy.

CONSPIRATORIAL DESIGN

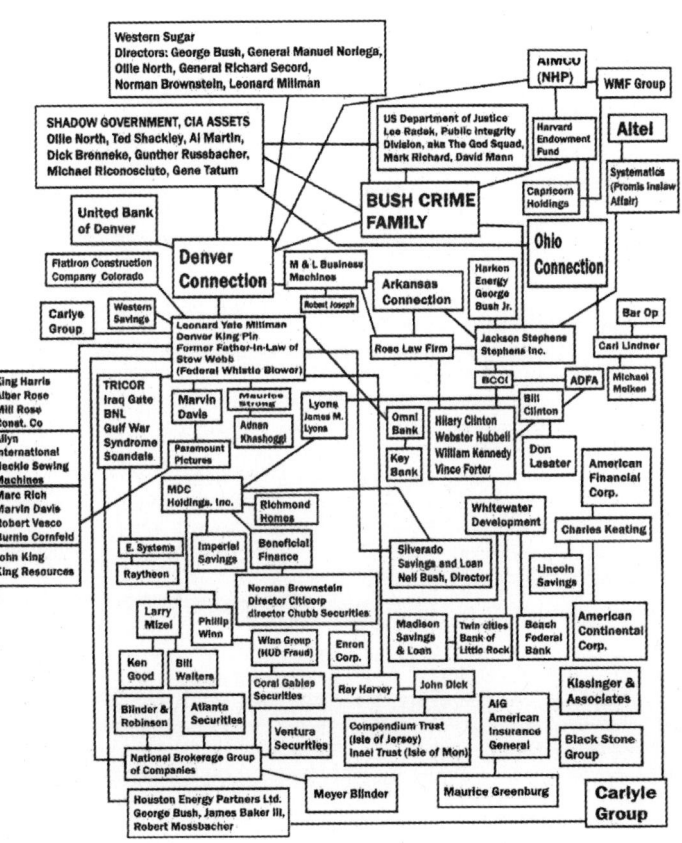

fig. 4

CONNECTING THE DOTS

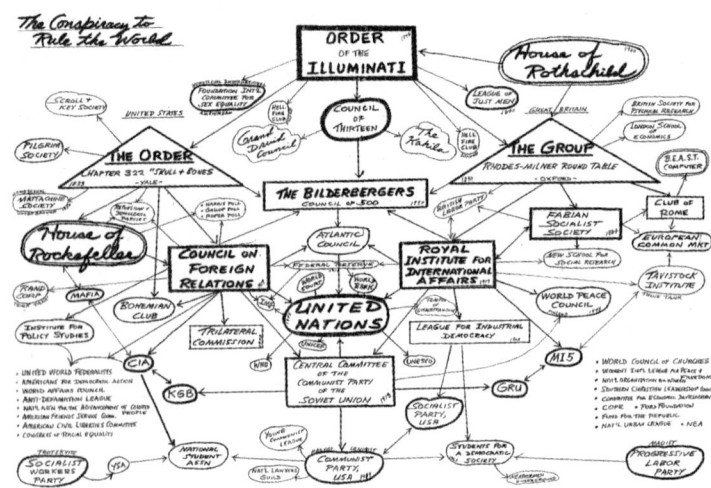

fig. 5

CONSPIRATORIAL DESIGN

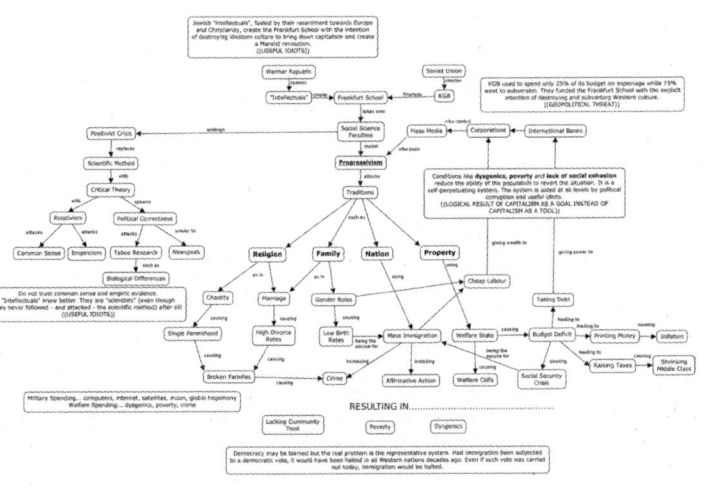

fig. 6

CONNECTING THE DOTS

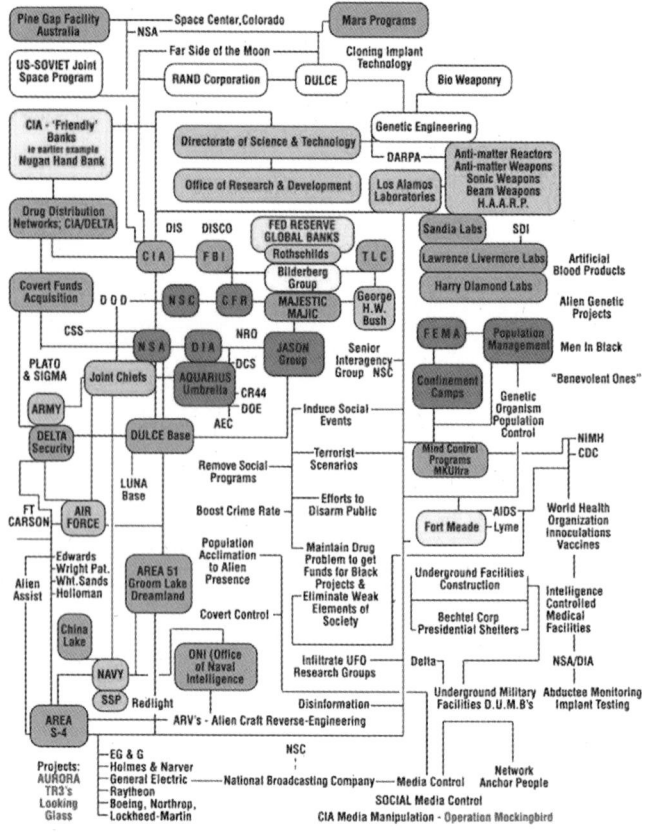

fig. 7

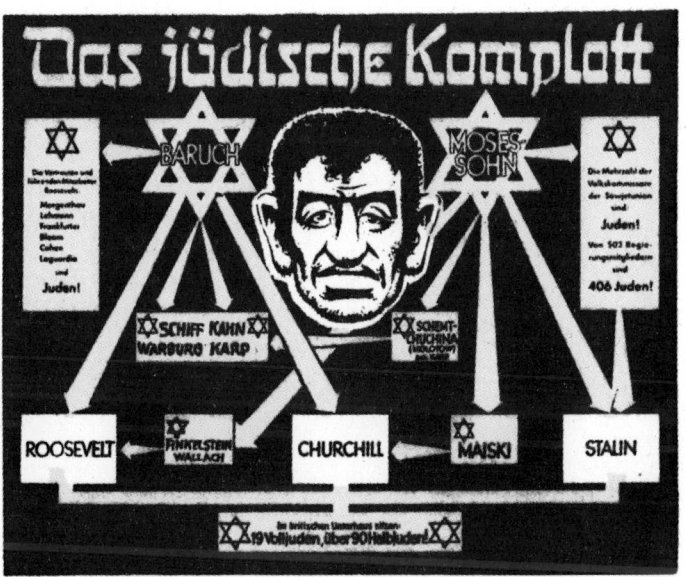

fig. 8

CONNECTING THE DOTS

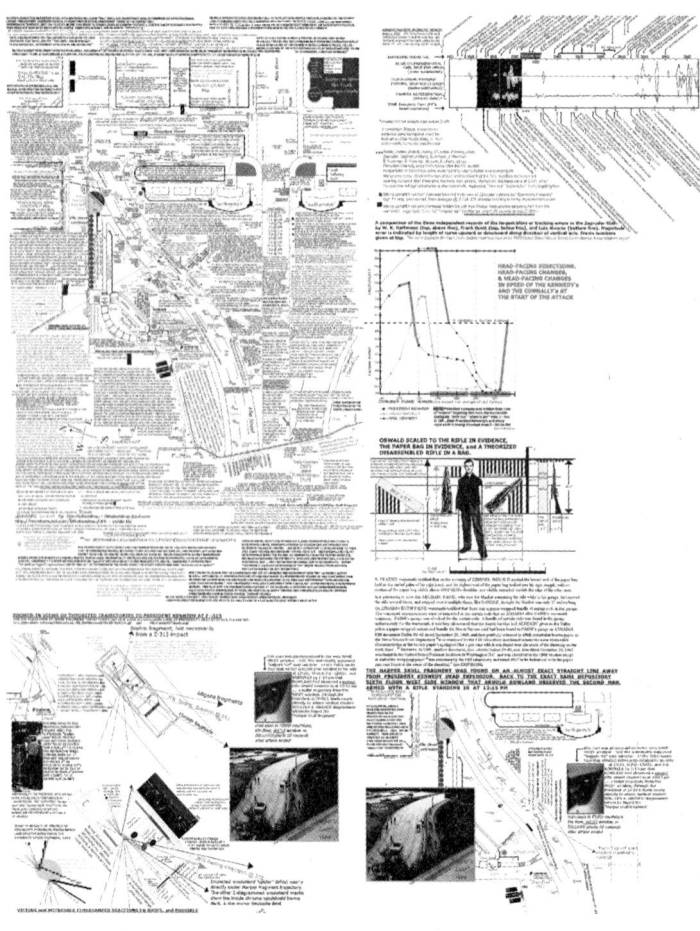

fig. 9

CONSPIRATORIAL DESIGN

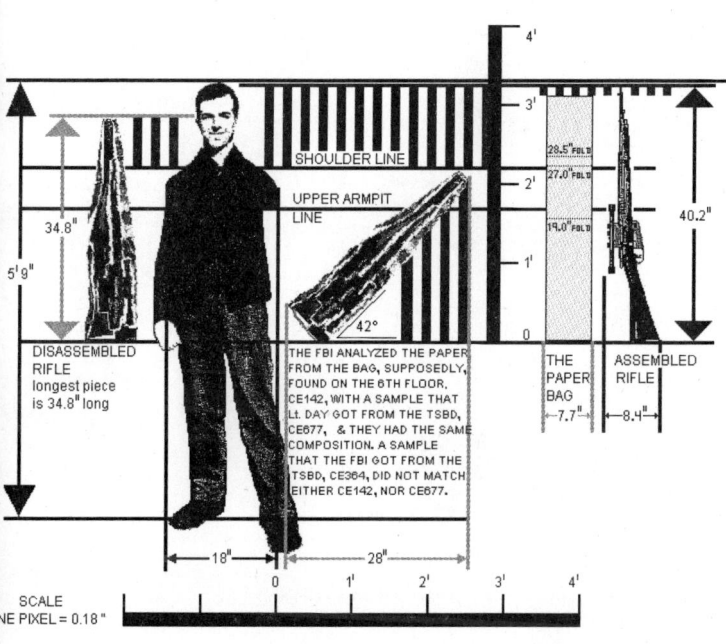

Detail from fig. 9

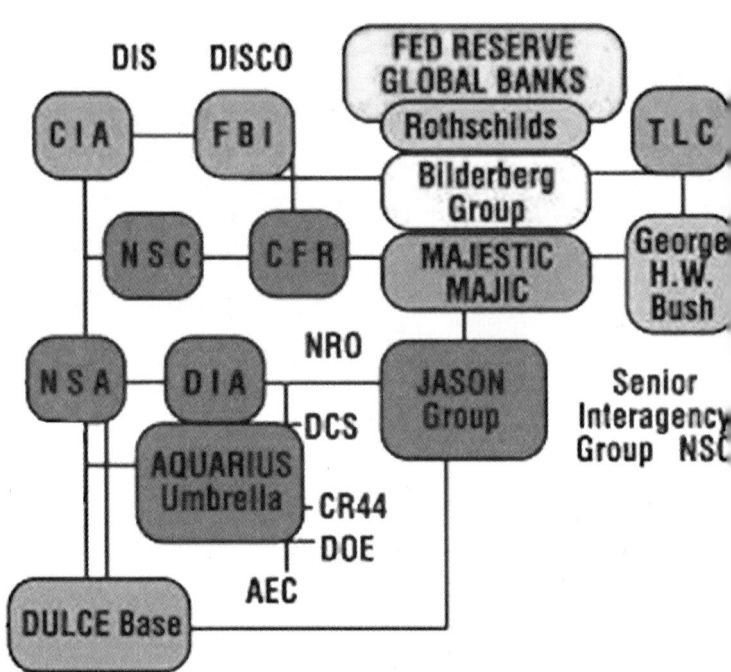

Detail from fig. 7

CONSPIRATORIAL DESIGN

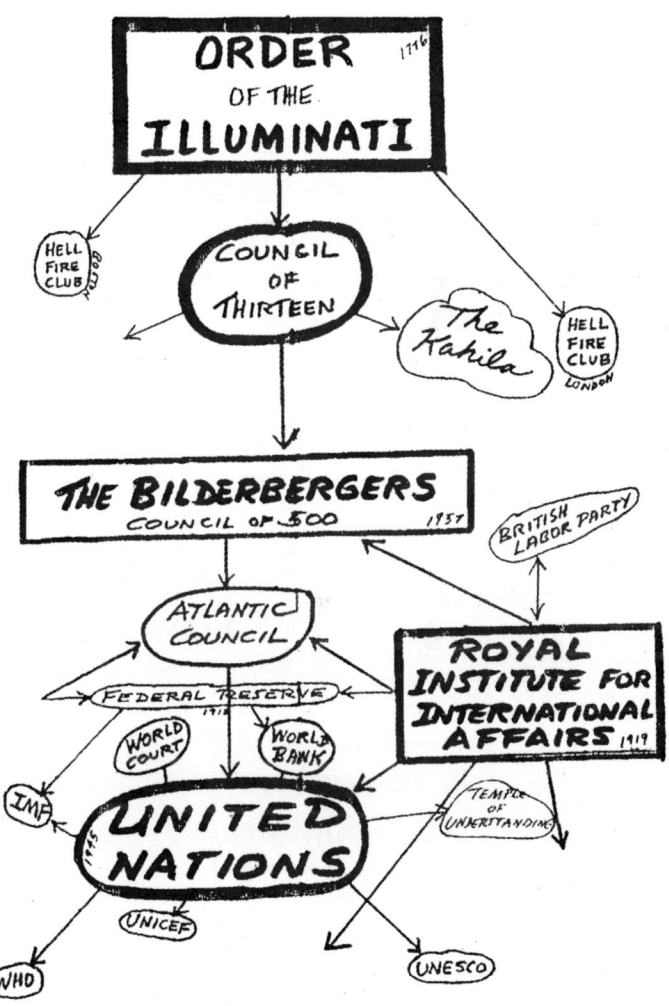

Detail from fig. 5

CONNECTING THE DOTS

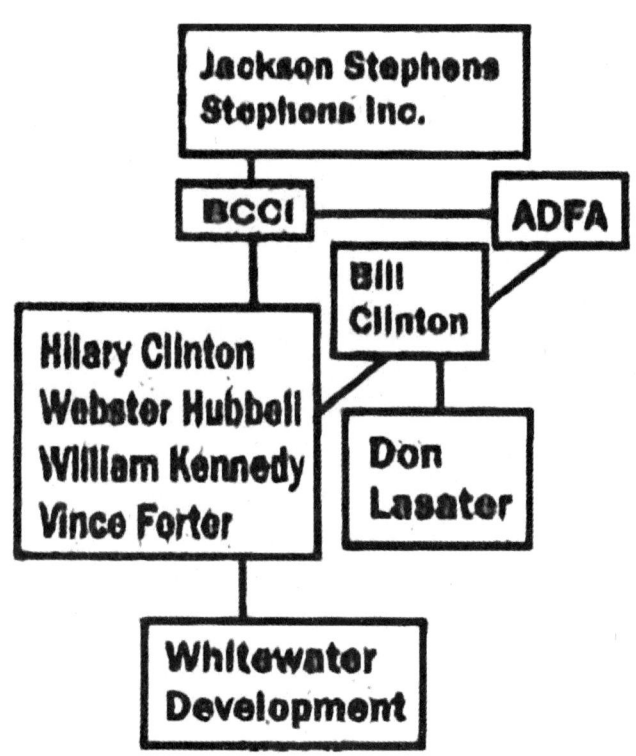

Detail from fig. 4

CONSPIRATORIAL DESIGN

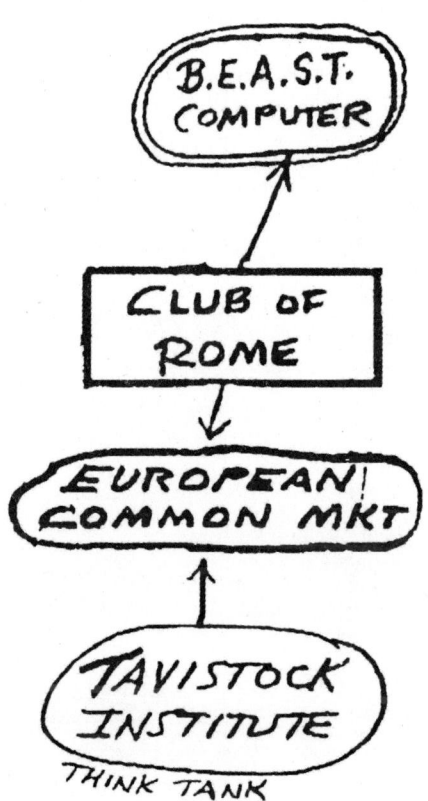

Detail from fig. 5

CONNECTING THE DOTS

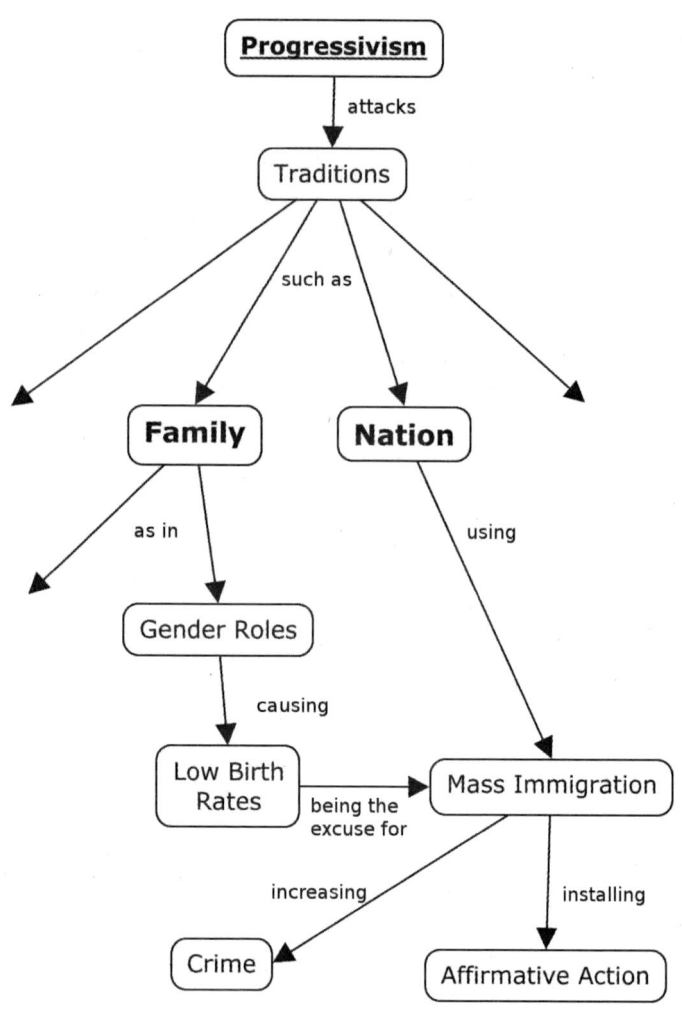

Detail from fig. 6

CONSPIRATORIAL DESIGN

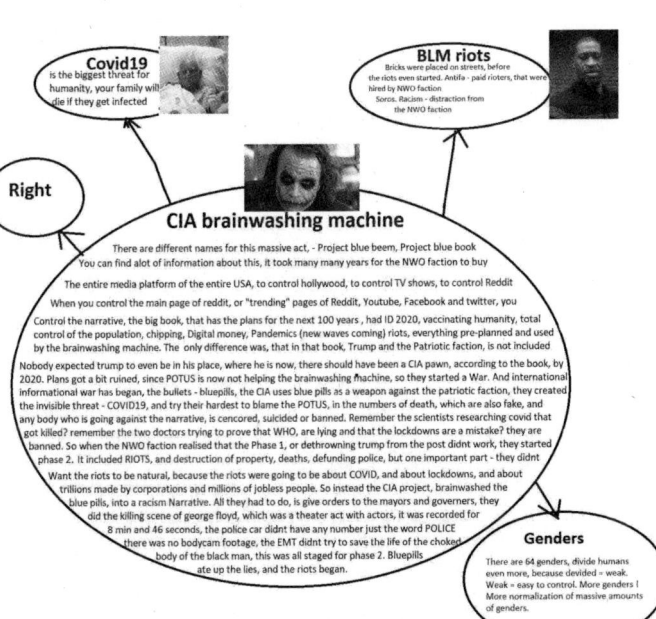

Detail from fig. 2

CONNECTING THE DOTS

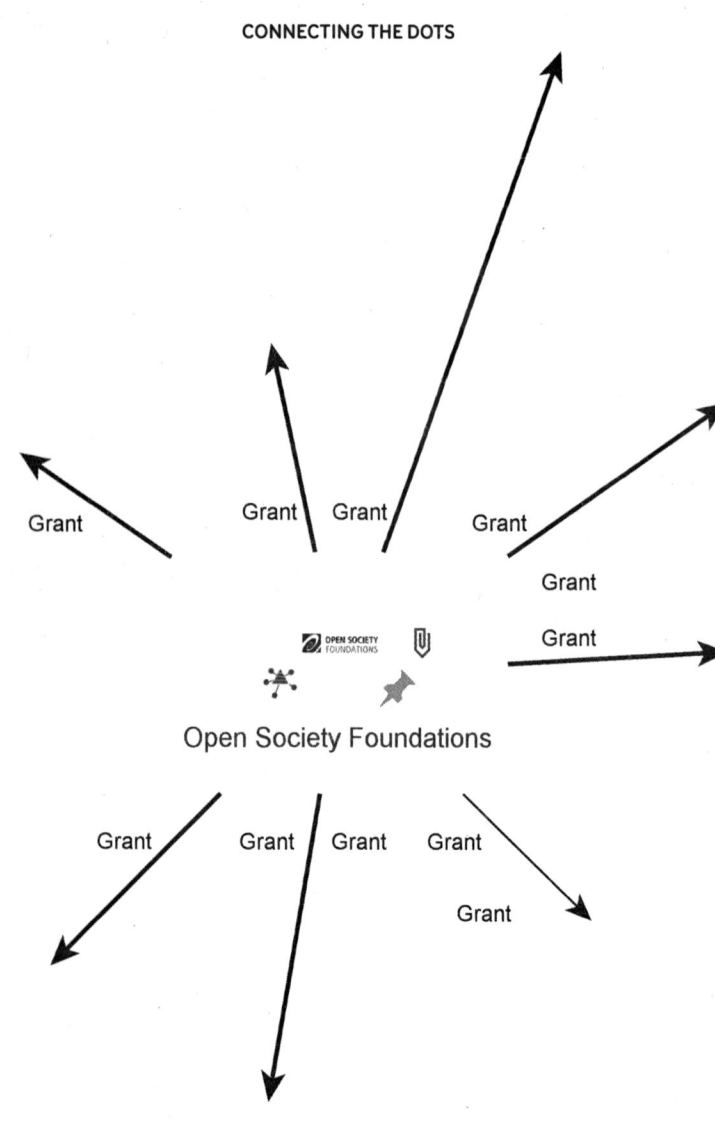

Detail from fig. 3

CONSPIRATORIAL DESIGN

God

Opposition of the SATAN worshippers. Religion might be another maze for the minds of bluepills to seek knowledge that they will never find because all the real knowledge is hidden in different close private libraries of the NWO and Vatican, but as long as they dont worship satan and they dont sacrifice childen, to moloch i would prefer the GOD people over that Satan people, as my allies. Also the Patriotic faction is strongly worshipping god. No additional infromation needed, its a choice of every single individual to believe or not.

Patriotic (USA) faction

Currently the strongest faction of opposition against the CIA faction. . JFK junior was a good friend of donald trump. And just like JFK, trump has a mission to get rid of the corrupt CIA pawns
inside of the USA government. He has been planning this for more than 20 years, they want to regain power over USA back, they worship god, they do not like the darkness of this world, they do not allow children to be raped and killed, they do not worship Satan.

The entire NWO faction hates the Patriotic faction, because Trump is doing everything against them, he defunded WHO, which was in control of the Gates foundation, he is against china having too much power over USA, he is trying to get rid of the "swamp". While the blue pills are only creating hate against him, because the CIA brainwashing project is moving a narrative, where the CIA pawns are being shown as "the best people on earth" and trump as the WORST. The CIA cannot assasinate him, because those are the rules of the game, especially when Trump has a very strong Death Switch.

Politics or not, god or devil, if you atleast dont like watching a child being beheaded on camera, while still alive, then you should not be against the Patriotic faction. They are plenty of flaws, alot of reasons to hate, but the CIA faction does way worse and way darker things. Like 9/11, killing millions of children and creating racism and riots.

Why do you think trump pronounced Antifa instantly, a terrorist organisastion? Because trump has thousands of red pills working in the intel, and in the military, they know about the factions, they know everthything.

if trump loses this war, and patriotic faction will fall, the NWO progression of the book, will continue

Trump does not have the ability to speak with the redpills, so he has to communicate with the blue pills, even when the CIA faction using reporters attacks him with questions that only feed the brainwashing machine of CIA, but not the redpilled people, so he has to be really careful on what he says. Sometimes its code words for the redpilled, sometimes its signs, but mostly he is trying to communicate with the Bluepills, not with us.
For communicating with the redpills, he uses hidden networks, like the Q anon.

Detail from fig. 2

CONNECTING THE DOTS

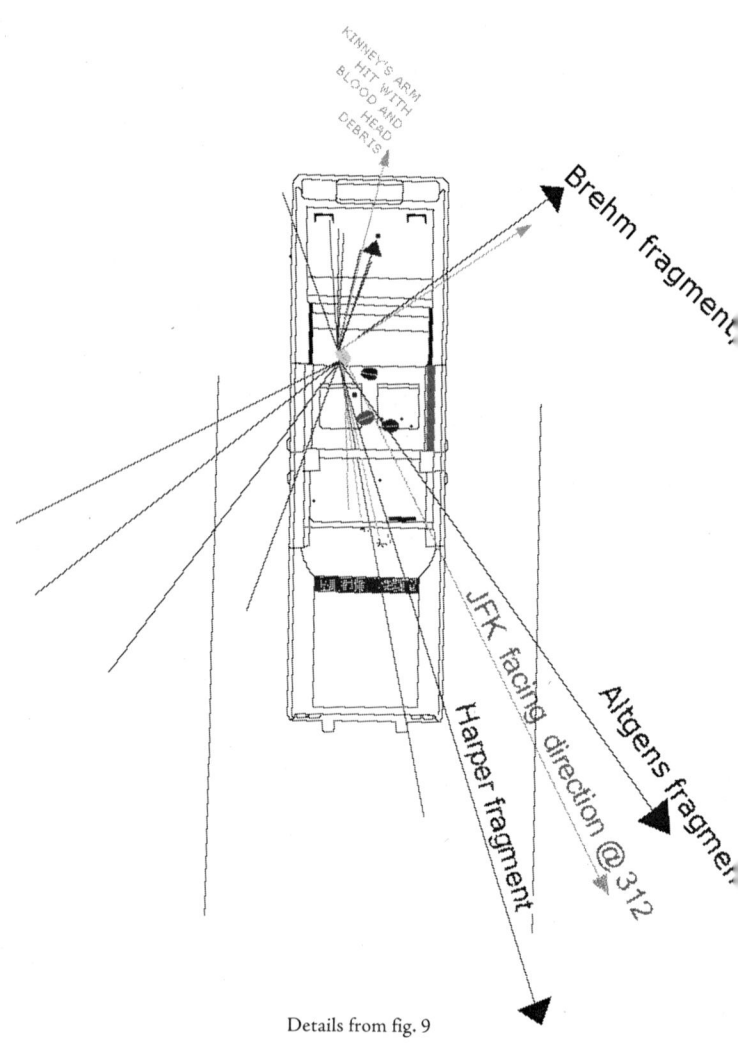

Details from fig. 9

CONSPIRATORIAL DESIGN

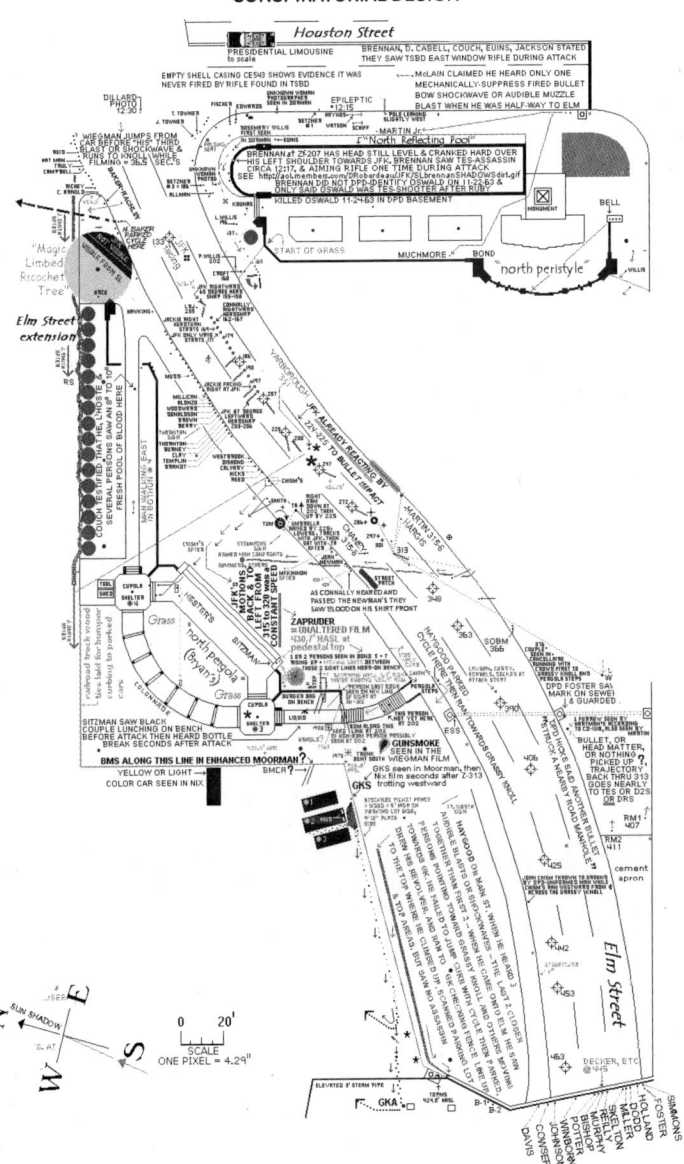

CONNECTING THE DOTS

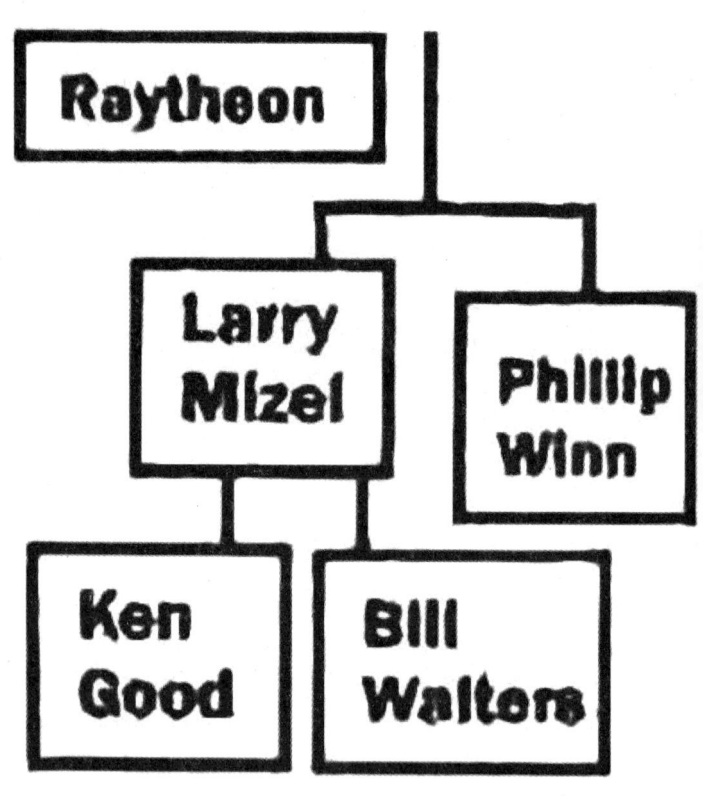

Detail from fig. 4

CONSPIRATORIAL DESIGN

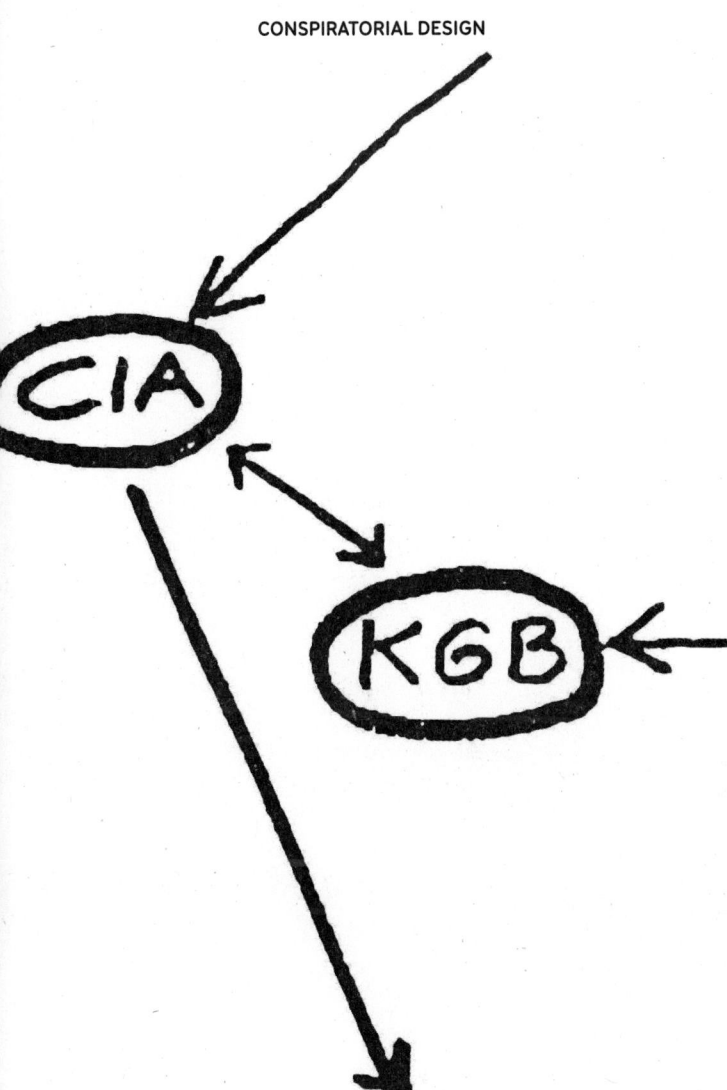

Detail from fig. 5

PART II.
DRAWING THE BORDERS: US AND THEM

A. HOW TO DRAW A LINE
B. DARK PESSIMISM
C. BREATHING TOGETHER

CONSPIRATORIAL DESIGN

A.
HOW TO DRAW A LINE

A typical conspiratorial trope is the presence of a nebulous "them": "That's what *they* want you to think". Of course that is a consequence of the fact that, like in every political narrative, it is useful to create an opponent. But the inherent indefiniteness of conspiracy theories generates an always mutable "them" contrasting an always mutable "us". The "us" are whoever participates in the theory and the "them" are a set of chosen agents (usually wealthy influential public figures) together with whoever tries to oppose the theory. This creates a sort of spy-like sense of suspicion: if you are actively trying to deconstruct the theory it must be because you have some sort of interest in doing it (the impostor could be among us). In John Carpenter's movie *They Live*[13] the main character realizes, by looking at the world through a pair of special sunglasses, that some people are actually part of a secret society of evil aliens that live concealed among humans forcing them to consume and obey thanks to subliminal messages. The movie, besides parodying and denouncing the consumeristic society, created one of the most iconic representations of the paranoid anxiety of a social menace conspiring in plain sight, living among us (being us!). With the success and the diffusion of contemporary conspiracy theories, a similar sense of anxiety grew among those who recognized the phenomenon as a great social threat and started wondering if conspiratorial

---

13   *They Live*, directed by John Carpenter, 1988.

fantasies were also haunting their friends and family. Even without the need to refer to the definitions given previously, the majority of people probably have a quite precise idea of what a conspiracy theory is. What I think is harder to define is *who* is a conspiracy theorist. Since the creation of these narratives is not a linear process, but rather the result of a chaotic collective storytelling game, it's not really possible to identify the theorist in the creator, nor in the believers, since there is not a precise shared belief. It's easy (and often politically useful) to create a dichotomy between a rational side and a foolish one. "Conspiratorial mentality" is a concept that has been weaponized to dismiss any anti-establishment instance, depicting an ideal political opposition as a homogeneous group of extremist fools with tinfoil on their heads. But reality is, as always, more nuanced. The baseline to understand when speaking about conspiracy theories is that we all have biases and that being aware of them is not enough to escape their effects. We all are constantly trying to confirm our assumptions, and this does not represent a fault in the well-functioning of our brains. It just means that our brain is working "well", as it descends from an evolutionary-convenient way to make cognitive work more efficient. Illusory pattern-seeking mechanisms and adaptive conspiracism (the tendency of humans to prefer to identify a possible menace, when in doubt, rather than none) are attitudes to which everyone is more or less subject. Besides that, we should also consider that a bias does not necessarily lead to a wrong conclusion (even a broken clock is right twice a day). One bias that is worth mentioning when it comes to conspiracy theories is the "proportionality bias": if something big happened, something big must have caused it. This kind of bias is what leads us to look for the world-scale origins of world-scale problems. Think of how naive it sounded to many people when at the beginning of Covid-19's outburst one would say there was no evidence to state the pandemic was caused by a geopolitical accident rather than a coincidental infection. By stressing how biases are the first common ground shared with conspiracy theorists, I don't want to conclude that everybody is always equally conspiratorial, but rather that I don't believe conspiracy theorists exist. What I mean by this is that I think that "conspiracy theorists" as a category is not very useful, as it's not possible to identify clearly who is this mysterious social group that believes in conspiracy theories. It's easy and reassuring to reduce it to the stereotypical image of the club of lunatic flat-earthers. If that were the case we would be talking about a handful of people with no political relevance, and not of the endemic phenomenon we are witnessing. What I see are rather minds wanting to think conspiratorially incentivized by the tools they have at their disposal and, at the same time, people with interests in exploiting their behaviors pretending to be part of them.

Designers are particularly vulnerable to the issues of conspiratorial thinking, as our job often consists of processing a lot of information, mediating it, and trying to synthesize it in order to produce an output that is emotionally appealing and narratively coherent. For example, a communication designer usually works by receiving a brief made of the goals of the commissioner, mixed with all kinds of more or less precise information, values, and ideas, to which they are asked to give order and use to come up with an original, coherent and compelling vision. Looking for patterns, and hunting new connections, is exactly what we are asked to do all the time. Let's take a tool of information design that can be used in such a process: network visualization. It would be a stretch to find something inherently conspiratorial in it. But let's consider an example of network visualization that we can still fully recognize as an information design project like the diagrams contained in *Atlas of Agendas* by Bureau d'Études.[14] In that case, we could start seeing some similarities, at least with the intention of revealing hidden webs of control. We could cite also Mark Lombardi, whose diagrams are often rightfully referenced as an investigative use of information design and taught in design schools as a historicized figure. In the case of Lombardi, the border becomes even fuzzier, as the mysteries surrounding the investigation by the FBI about his diagrams and the alleged unclear circumstances around his suicide, make his work a reference in design as much as in conspiracy theories. Lastly, if we take the work of a visual artist like Suzanne Treister, the distinction between visual design

14   Bureau d'Études, *An Atlas of Agendas: Mapping the Power, Mapping the Commons*, 2019.

and conspiracy theories becomes almost impossible (I was specifically denied to include images of her work for fear that the association with conspiracy theories was misleading, so look it up and evaluate for yourself), as the intentions, the themes, the style, and the symbology used in her diagrams, make her a perfect example of the overlapping of the two worlds. Where does design end and conspiracy theories begin? These three examples are not random. I chose them because I found them often referenced in online conspiracy environments, which interestingly enough are not making distinctions in the first place, and consider them valid inspirations and sources for research.

The point I'm trying to make by zooming in on this blurriness is double. In the first place, there is an issue with making a clear distinction between us and them: how do we draw a line? And secondly, what is it that we are trying to achieve by drawing this line?

B.
DARK OPTIMISM

Since conspiracy theories started becoming a common cultural phenomenon more and more people started to wonder how to approach this growing mass of "unconventional-truths-believers" and how to collocate them politically. These attempts happened hand in hand with the emergence of populist movements in many different countries, mutually comparable for the generic anti-establishment desires, not always connected with more traditional ideological positions. Once again, Trump's administration is probably the most recognizable example, representing not a classic republican presidency, but a whole new kind of weird far-right populism. What emerged is that it can be quite a challenge to embed conspiracy theories followers in a political movement, as they seem to be shifting their values around extremely quickly, probably in an attempt to make them consistent with the ever-changing nature of their beliefs. While conspiracy theories have been widely instrumentalized by far-right movements, some attempts have come from the opposite side of the political compass to find a way to include them. Different theoretical proposals emerged from left political areas to try to identify what good or at least powerful narrative force can be reframed for better purposes inside conspiracy theories. The main theorist who laid the ground for this kind of attempt was Fredric Jameson who in *The Geopolitical Aesthetic*[15] describes conspiracy theories as "poor people's cognitive mapping". By "cognitive mapping" he means the capacity to create a mental image of social structures, collocate oneself in it, and navigate them. Jameson proposes the necessity to arrive at what he calls "the aesthetic of cognitive mapping", which is a means to represent, through artistic objects (in his case cinema, but it can apply to design as well), the totality of the complex social structures in order for the individual to see themselves as part of it, and eventually, hopefully, find a way to destructure it. In this conception

15 Fredric Jameson, *The Geopolitical Aesthetic: Cinema and Space in the World System*, 1995.

Jameson interprets conspiracy theorists as people who are working in the right direction, trying to visualize a totality, but failing to recognize the whole for what it really is: capitalism. In the previously quoted lecture *Dark Optimism: Conspiratorial Styles of Reasoning for the Biosphere*, Robert Pietrusko adopts a similar theoretical framework. After documenting the traces of a conspiratorial approach in many architecture and design projects, he argues how conspiratorial thinking can be read from an optimistic perspective as the ability to see the world as an immense interconnected environment, where new governance systems need to be imagined to keep up with the incoming global crises, such as climate change. With this interpretation, an almost paradoxical form of optimism emerges from conspiracy theories. The classic conspiratorial conception of "the world order" (intended as a designed system that works like a well-oiled gear in which large-scale organizations manage to control everything, even to a microscopic level) is dystopian only if you imagine it pursuing values that are opposite to yours. But it can also represent, for example, a socialist utopia. Pietrusko suggests to refuse a dichotomy between an "enlightened us vs a misguided them". Instead, he proposes that conspiracy theories can be an example for speculative designers to be more radical and ambitious in their work of reality-building. While finding Pietrusko's lecture remarkable and inspiring, I don't share the optimism (I guess that makes me a dark pessimist). In the first place, I don't think that existing conspiracy theories are necessarily fundamentally opposed to socialism. An interesting example of this is Jacob Angeli, the QAnon "shaman" who became a symbolic figure in the attack on Capitol Hill. In his book *One Mind At A Time: A Deep State of Illusion*[16] Angeli describes the utopia that will be achieved after the fall of the Deep State. What is fascinating is that the world he describes might be fuzzy and naive, but is definitely not an ultra-capitalistic conservative one. Instead, it has many progressive left ambitions such as universal public healthcare, high incomes for teachers, and the abolition of the death penalty. Of course, mine is not an apology of QAnon, which is in fact composed mainly of ultra-conservative white supremacists. On the contrary, what I mean is that the political problem with conspiracy theories goes deeper than the level of the adopted flags. Conspiracy theories are fascist in their methods even before then in their claims. The second reason why I don't share Pietrusko's dark optimism is that I am generally skeptical about the ability of design to "envision new worlds". I'm often not convinced by the claims of many projects, whether of design fiction or speculative design (let's use "critical design" as an umbrella term), about their ability to trigger in the audience the irrepressible instinct to collectively reconfigure our distorted present, simply because I don't see it happen. Speculative design is intentionally about made-up scenarios. The same definition of Speculative Design by

16 Jacob Angeli, *One Mind At A Time: A Deep State of Illusion*, 2020.

Anthony Dunne and Fiona Raby,[17] who coined it, is "an activity where conjecture is as good as knowledge". The issue is that this same conception doesn't stay confined to some specific design contexts but becomes part of every design practice that aspires to be perceived as elite in that it is more radically future-oriented. Like Afonso de Matos documents in his *Who can afford to be critical*[18] a recognizable feature of critical design projects is that the goal of many of them is to "raise awareness", as the presence of this same expression in numerous project descriptions testifies. The fact that design, and especially information design as we have seen, has some pedagogic intent comes as no surprise. The necessary premise of every form of information design is that there is some information that the designer must simplify before giving it to the uneducated audience. What interests me in relation to conspiracy theories is the tendency of many designers to bring that ambition deeper, assuming a "maieutic" role, not simply educating their audience but—borrowing a term from QAnon—"awakening" it. During my studies at Design Academy Eindhoven, I attended a lecture where a design studio described their work as "A practice that bypasses the established narratives about the present and future that create the hypnosis of normality". I found that the description succinctly captured a sort of unconscious assumption widespread

---

17 Anthony Dunne and Fiona Raby, *Speculative Everything: Design, Fiction, and Social Dreaming*, 2013.
18 Afonso de Matos, *Who Can Afford to Be Critical? An Inquiry into What We Can't Do Alone, as Designers, and into What We Might Be Able to Do Together, as People*, 2022.

in the design field: the world is hypnotized by lies (in this case about the present and the future, so everything except the past) but designers are able to tear through the veil of Maya. The myth of the awakening is innate in every conspiratorial narrative as testified for example by the great diffusion in the right-wing American political discourse of the expressions "red-pilled/blue-pilled" (referencing *The Matrix*) to divide the world between independent thinkers and slaves of mainstream narratives. Thinking of being in the position to educate the masses might sound wishful, but believing that your role is to awaken consciences almost reaches a god complex. Jameson's "aesthetic of cognitive mapping" would also have a pedagogic intent, but Jameson himself expressed how the final representation of the totality that he described was ultimately unachievable.[19] What I want to state here is that, while in terms of principle I share many of the reframing proposals on conspiracy theories that I encountered, I feel they never manage to escape the same paternalistic dichotomy of "enlightened us vs a misguided them" denounced by Pietrusko. In my opinion, for designers to have a clear perspective on conspiracy theories, we must first acknowledge design's inherent conspiratorial nature. "We" are "them".

Let's try now to push the boundaries of my "dark pessimism" by looking at an interesting case study. Wandering on conspiracy threads on Reddit I stumbled across a fascinating image. A user shared a poster

---

19   Alberto Toscano and Jeff Kinkle, *Cartographies of the Absolute*, 2015

he made on the subreddit "r/SaturnStormCube", a space dedicated to "exposing the occult agenda of the global cabal". The poster is called *Abstraction*[20] and, even if words don't do it justice, we can describe it as a messy hyper-dense diagram that denounces the existence of techniques of mass mind control and illustrates their functioning. It is published on the personal website of the user, where one can find various theories of the author presented in the form of an obscure website, where walls of text, densely packed diagrams, and street-taken pictures mix in an investigative game for the user, who needs to dive in the rabbit hole of the content to access secret sections. The website is also connected to other friend websites. There is for example *Superpredator*,[21] a seemingly dadaist project, with a disruptive tone and a brutal aesthetic, suggesting the production of an open collaborative zine with some pretty strong claims, such as "SUPERPREDATOR *is the premier publication for* HYPERJOURNALISM *and* PSEUDOPSYCHOSIS! *The final and last source of real news in the entire world!*" or "ADD WHATEVER YOU LIKE! REMOVE WHATEVER YOU DON'T LIKE! *Change anything you want!* IT ONLY MAKES IT MORE TRUE!". Most of these interconnected websites are dominated by a Webcore aesthetic[22]—a reevaluation of the 90's internet. Some of them are part of the "Wired Collective", a group of users inter-

---

20 *Abstraction*, https://sitcomtheory.org/ABSTRACTION
21 *SUPERPREDATOR*, https://superpredator.zone
22 Jenna Wortham, *The Death and Life of Great American GeoCities*, The New York Times Magazine, February 27, 2015.

ested in *Serial Experiments Lain*,[23] a late 90's anime revolving around a girl (Lain) and her connection to a virtual reality network known as "The Wired". The fact that conspiracy environments show an interest in Serial Experiments Lain doesn't come as a surprise. First of all because in this context it's perfectly consistent with the early Internet nostalgia; and secondly because it is a work that—together with other works of the same period, like *The Matrix* and *Existez*—created a representation of a kind of "digital gnosticism"(i.e., material reality is a deception and technology gives us access to a higher dimension). What I find more surprising is the level of dedication and graphic experimentation these websites showcase, without the drive of a commercial purpose or large exposure. Works such as the "Abstraction" poster impressed me for several reasons. First of all for the initial impact given by the level of of intricacy. It clearly draws inspiration from other similar older works of conspiracy diagrams that we'll see later on (like the ones of Dylan Louis Monroe), and if possible, it puts them on steroids. From a graphic design perspective, I was genuinely impressed by the spontaneous stylistic choices, such as using 3D reflections on typography hinting at contemporary trends. Besides, the experience of deciphering a black and white graphic composition that is at the same time obscure, grungy and symbolically allusive, evoked a similarity for me with works such as those of Avocado Ibuprofen and Boot Boyz Biz. The work also suggests a certain graphic design culture by featuring

---

23 Giovanni Padua, *Serial Experiments Lain e le radici psichiche della cybercultura gnostica*, L'Indiscreto, 2024.

Gestalt experiments. The author doesn't have a design background, but the dedication to the project gives it in my opinion the same dignity and aesthetic value as other forms of "vernacular" design. I find it fascinating how many of the websites that are part of the Wired Collective, if given the right context, could easily pass as provocative graduation projects in a design school.

I wanted to mention these cases because they suggest me this idea: If attacking power structures and speculating on alternative realities become the main guidelines for good design, without a backbone of analytical precision and without proposing any realistic intervention, then we can push Pietrusko's "dark optimism" even further: conspiracy theories not only inspire design but surpass it. They are more radical, more imaginative, they circulate more, and in some cases they are even more visually experimental.

C.
BREATHING TOGETHER:

In his 1988 novel *Foucault's Pendulum*, Umberto Eco tells the story of three young editors who create a mock conspiracy theory called "The Plan" as a literary game. The Plan weaves together various historical and esoteric elements into an elaborate narrative. The three become involved in the story to the point that they can't tell reality from fiction and end up entangled in a web of occult and historical mysteries:

> When we traded the results of our fantasies, it seemed to us—and rightly—that we had proceeded by unwarranted associations, by shor-

tcuts so extraordinary that, if anyone had accused us of really believing them, we would have been ashamed. We consoled ourselves with the realization—unspoken, now, respecting the etiquette of irony—that we were parodying the logic of our Diabolicals. But during the long intervals in which each of us collected evidence to produce at the plenary meetings, and with the clear conscience of those who accumulate material for a medley of burlesques, our brains grew accustomed to connecting, connecting, connecting everything with everything else, until we did it automatically, out of habit. I believe that you can reach the point where there is no longer any difference between developing the habit of pretending to believe and developing the habit of believing.[24]

Among the many themes in *Foucault's Pendulum*, this passage allows me to highlight two elements that I consider central to conspiratorial design: the role of the community and its relationship with fiction and parody. As for the community, even the etymology of conspiracy suggests that *to conspire* is something you do with someone else ("Conspiracy": from Latin *cum spirare* = breathing together). The community serves as a constant source of both signs and interpretations. From these one can extrapolate just the needed confirmations, reinforcing one's beliefs without the necessity to ever doubt them. At the same time, the

---

24 Umberto Eco, *Foucault's Pendulum*, 1988.

community is necessary to keep together the ambiguity on the level of the parody, leaving the possibility for everybody to never declare to others (and to themselves) to what degree they are invested in their beliefs. Or in other words the community keeps together the suspension of disbelief. To explain this better I think that an interesting and useful notion is that of *kayfabe*.[25] "Kayfabe" is a term originally and primarily used in professional wrestling to indicate the portrayal of staged events or storylines as genuine and unscripted. In the modern age though, kayfabe is not to be intended as a hustle for the gullible audience, but rather as a two-sided agreement on the suspension of disbelief. If you go to a live professional wrestling match and start telling the cheering audience that the show is rigged, you will most likely look like an idiot. This is because kayfabe takes a step forward in terms of credulity compared to the usual suspension of disbelief. It involves the performers, the audience, and the organizers equally, at all times, inside and outside the stage, to not just enjoy the show *as if* it was real, but to get as close as possible to *make it* real. The unspoken agreement in professional wrestling is that, no matter to what degree you believe in what you are seeing, you are taking part in a collective alternate-reality game, where morality (the good wrestlers vs the villains) is displayed through violence. The violence may be fake, but the desire for a clash of moralities is very real. I find the notion of kayfabe interesting because it's localized in a very spe-

25   Brad Troemel, *The KAYFABE Report*, Patreon, August 2022.

cific social context, but it highlights a behavior that is not exclusive to professional wrestling, namely the use of ambiguity in collective parodies. Think for example of meme culture, and how many meme pages are based on not being explicit on how ironic the content is meant to be (it would be indeed pretty lame to see a meme page that specifies that they are being ironic). In this way through memes, we create a distance from the content that grants us a more acceptable "jester's privilege" (i.e. "I can say whatever I want because I'm joking… unless…?"). On the contrary, being the one person who asks to someone who is making a parody what they truly believe is a terrible position. It means to demand from somebody to take responsibility for their ideas by publicly acknowledging them and spoiling the fun for everybody else.

Coming back to our objects of study, how a form of kayfabe takes place in conspiracy theories is pretty evident. Exactly like professional wrestling, conspiracy theories are somehow a form of allegorical theatre.[26] The audience and the performers mix into one group of more or less participative and more or less aware, with people who fully believe the theory, others completely aware that it is fake and just want to have fun, and others who don't even ask themselves the question. The story's truthfulness becomes a completely irrelevant parameter as long as there is, inside of what is being told, a "core of truth".[27] The core of truth is an underlying truth that triggers the need for a

---

[26] This comparison was proposed in a lecture in 2019 by Wu Ming 1
[27] Wu Ming 1, *La Q Di Qomplotto: QAnon e Dintorni: Come Le Fantasie Di Complotto Difendono Il Sistema*, 2021.

conspiracy theory. For example, In the case of the conspiracy theories around 9/11, the core of truth is the fact that the US government has often acted in shady and dishonest ways, even damaging their own citizens, to pursue their geopolitical interests. The population's mistrust in their government needed a representation that, among many others, took the form of 9/11 conspiracy theories. The problem is that by criticizing conspiracy theories on 9/11, which are for the vast majority complete garbage, one often ends up being perceived as criticizing the core of truth, which instead can present valid critiques.

As for design, I see this kind of ambiguity take place among many research-based works. My impression is that many in the design field lack the analytical rigor, but more importantly the interest, to check the information. Exactly like in conspiracy theories, often in design, it is sufficient to recreate the sensation of research and of "criticality". In this, the role of the community is central as well. The design community produces knowledge without following any scientific procedure. I don't mean this is a problem per se since it would probably be very complicated, and maybe even unfruitful, to always apply rigorous scientific methods in a discipline where following intuition is often a more agile approach compared to an evidence-based one. This though tends to lead to a more "Darwinistic" diffusion of ideas in the design field, in the sense the fittest—the ones that bring a stronger narrative, or a more felt core of truth—will proliferate. This is where I see the kayfabe element in design. When a project tackles a core of truth, designers and design audience lose any interest in what is actually being proposed: the conclusion becomes irrelevant as long as *awareness* is being raised. A critique of this sort that I find meaningful is the one made by Greg Stone about Mark Lombardi in *Mark Lombardi: Global Networks*. Mark Lombardi was an artist who between the 1970s and the 1990s produced a series of drawings called "Narrative Structures" representing diagrams meant to expose the connections between various power-abusing agents. Even though Lombardi's works are extremely meticulously executed, they sometimes lack the rigor necessary to fully serve a spectator who would want to actually use his diagrams to investigate the topic in question and not just as aesthetical objects. Greg Stone puts it in this terms:

> Lombardi's drawings are like a pointillist work, best viewed from afar. From a distance you can see that a system has been revealed, but the closer you get to it the more invisible it becomes.[28]

The burden of analytical rigor shouldn't be just of the authors, but of the whole community, and the responsibility for an actual effective critique (when critique is the ambition of a design project) shouldn't be just expected from the designers but also demanded by the audience.

---

28 Robert Carleton Hobbs et al., *Mark Lombardi - Global Networks*, 2004.

CONSPIRATORIAL DESIGN

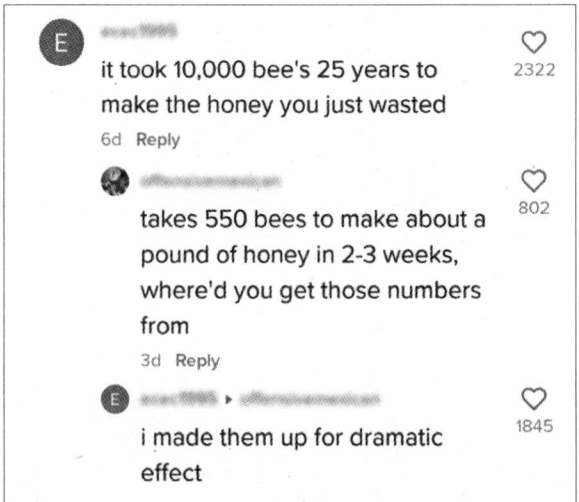

fig. 10   Source unknown.

DRAWING THE BORDERS

CONSPIRATORIAL DESIGN

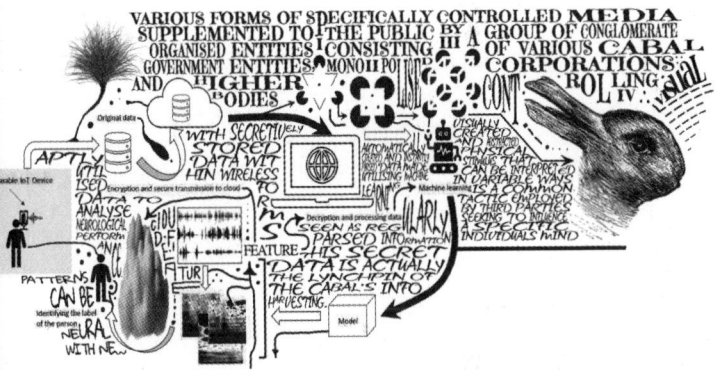

fig. 11   *Abstraction*, @farquhaad, 2024.
(Full image on the left page, detail on the right)

DRAWING THE BORDERS

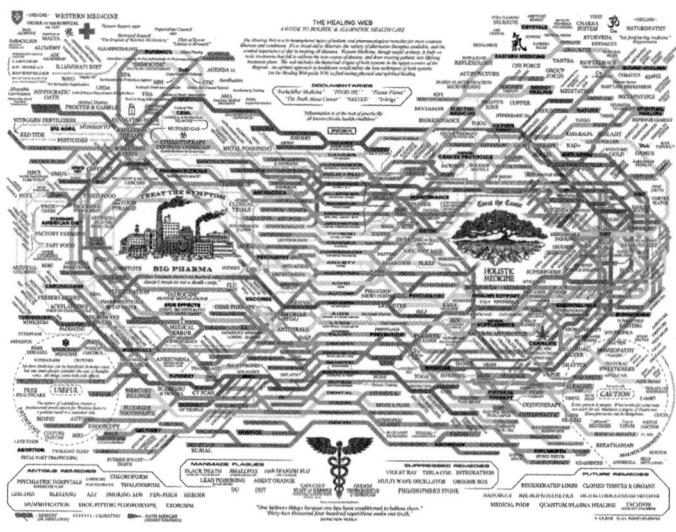

fig. 12 *Healing Web*, Dylan Louis Monroe, 2019.
Digital. 8.5 x 11 in. www.deepstatemappingproject.com

CONSPIRATORIAL DESIGN

fig. 13 Image from *https://superpredator.zone/*

DRAWING THE BORDERS

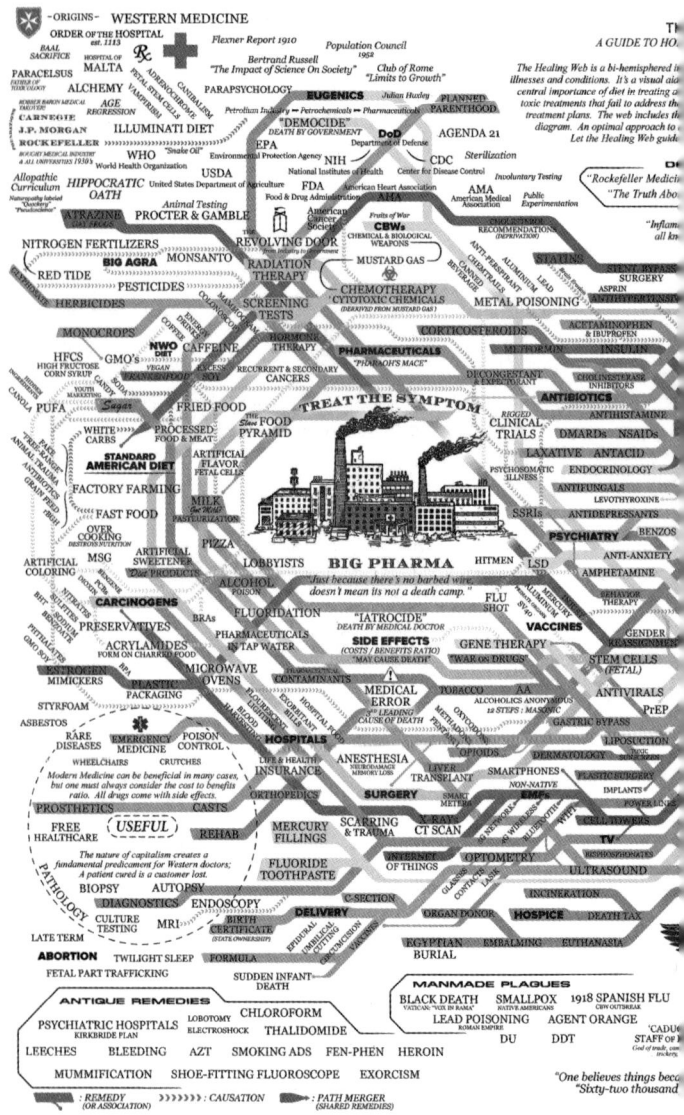

78

CONSPIRATORIAL DESIGN

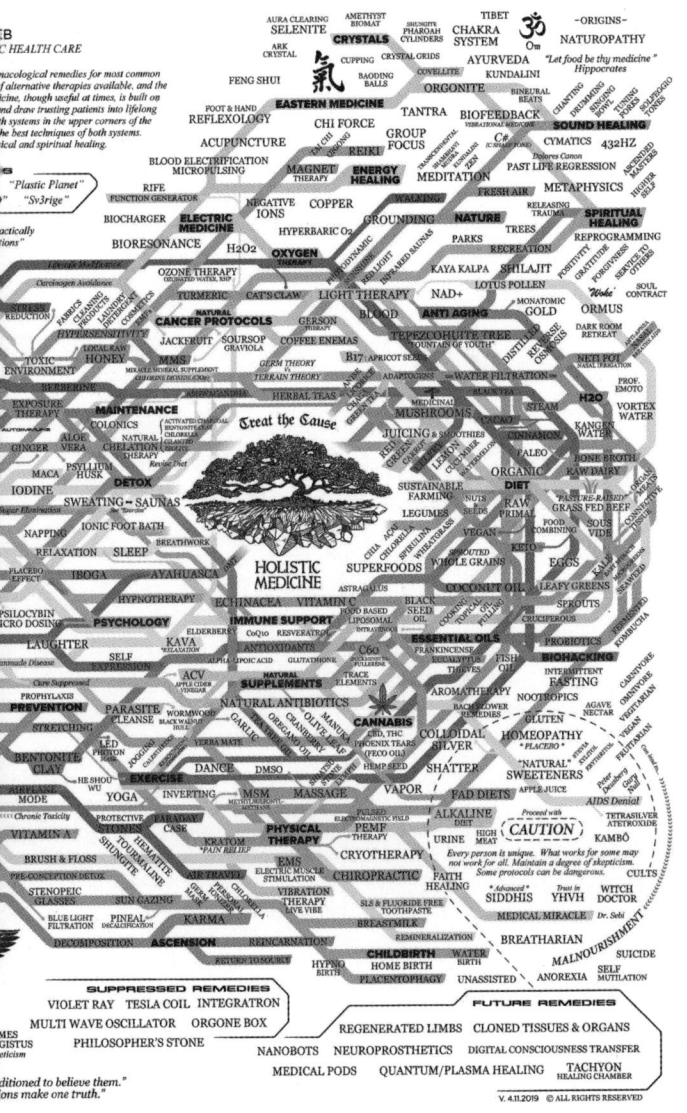

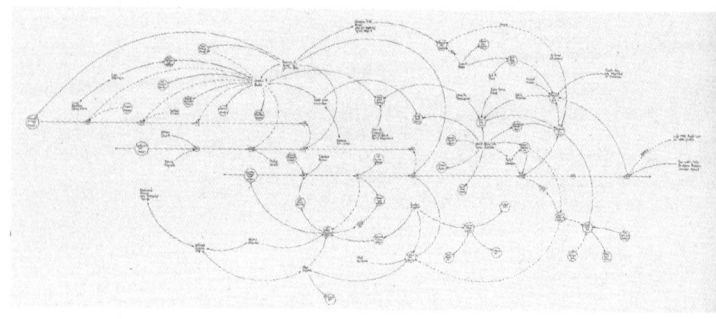

fig. 14   *Network Structure*, Mark Lombardi, 1979-1990.

CONSPIRATORIAL DESIGN

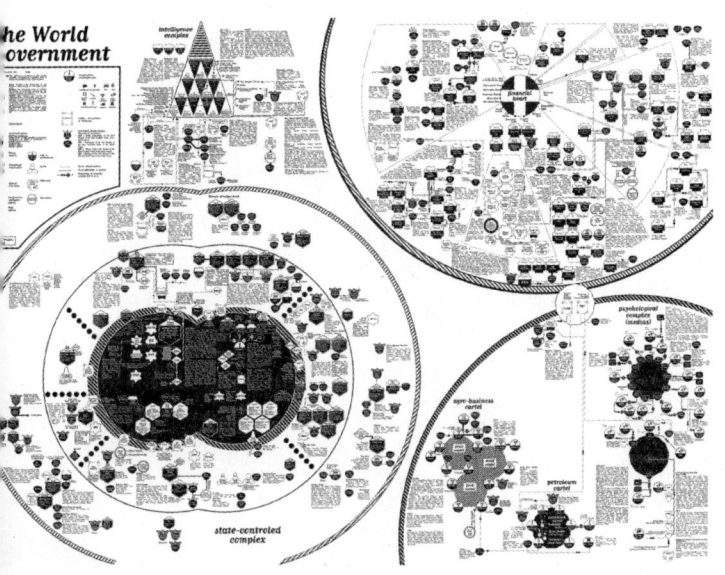

fig. 15   Diagram from *Atlas of Agendas* by Bureau d'Études, 2019.

fig. 16 Diagram by Craighton Berman, 2025

CONSPIRATORIAL DESIGN

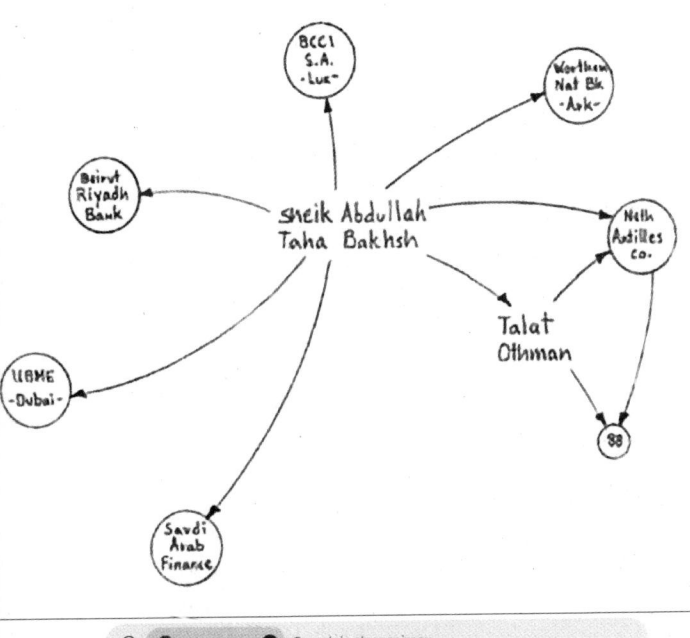

Top — detail from fig. 13

fig. 17 — Screenshot of a comment in a thread about Mark Lombardi, from the subreddit r/conspiracy.

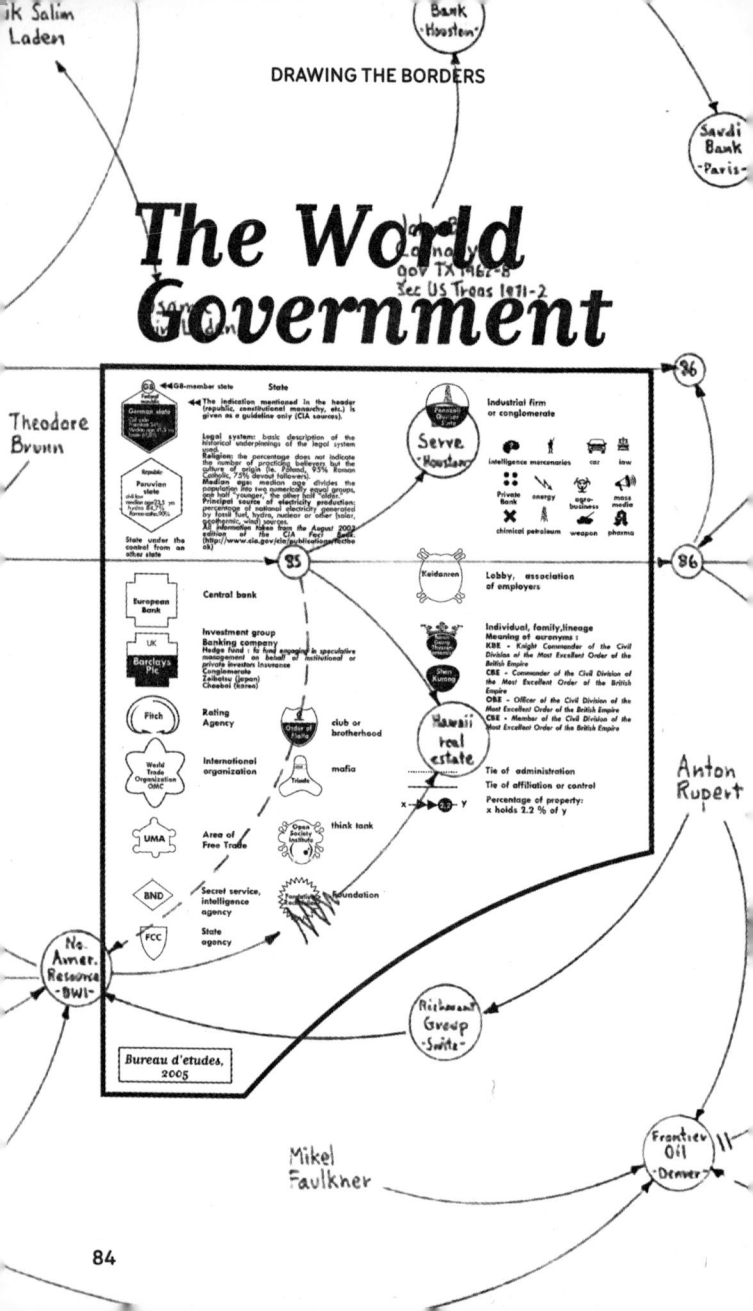

CONSPIRATORIAL DESIGN

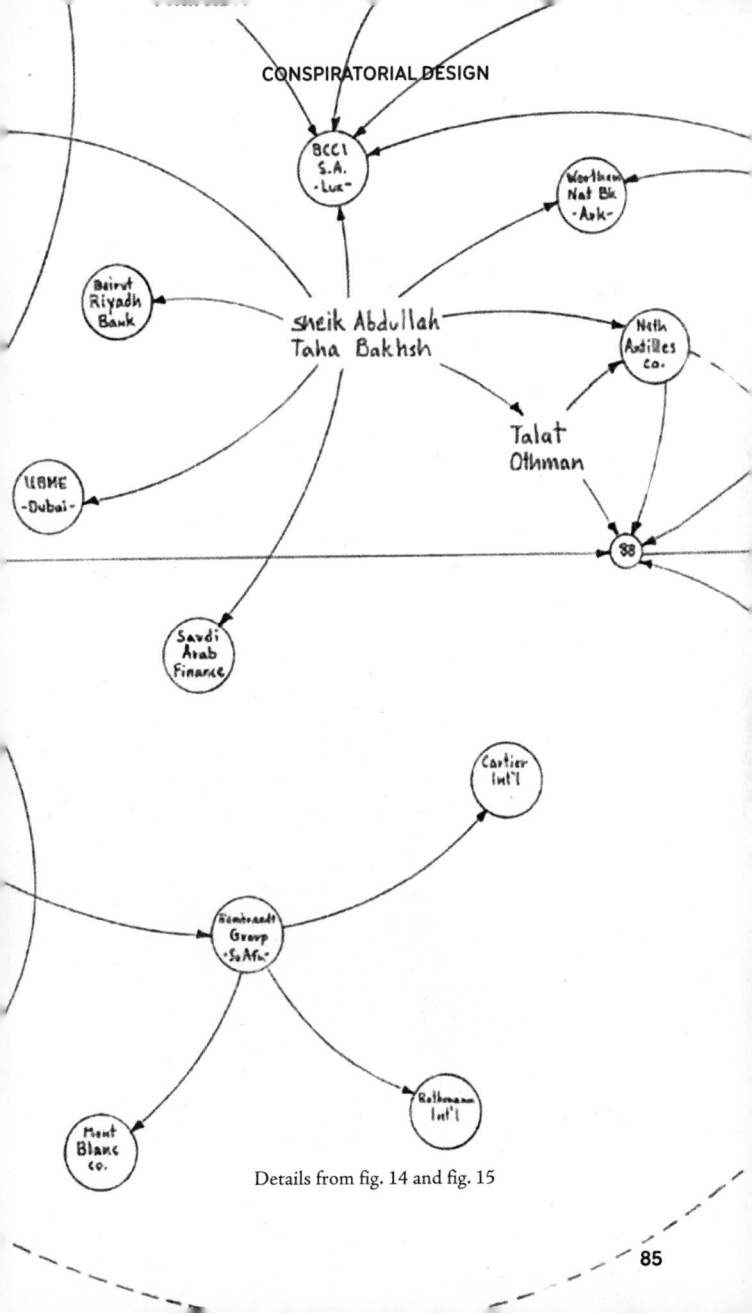

Details from fig. 14 and fig. 15

DRAWING THE BORDERS

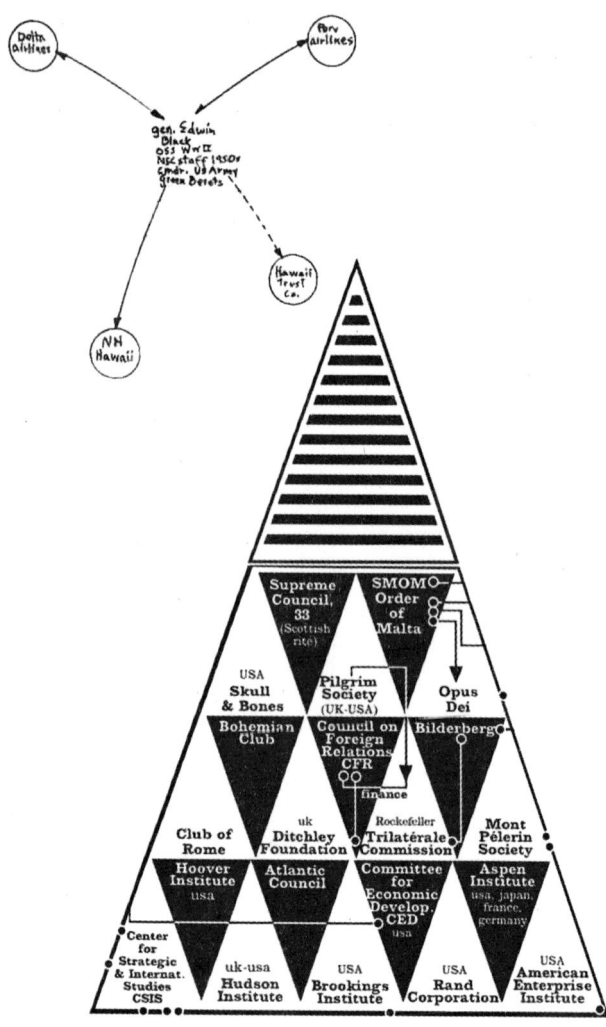

Details from fig. 14 and fig. 15

CONSPIRATORIAL DESIGN

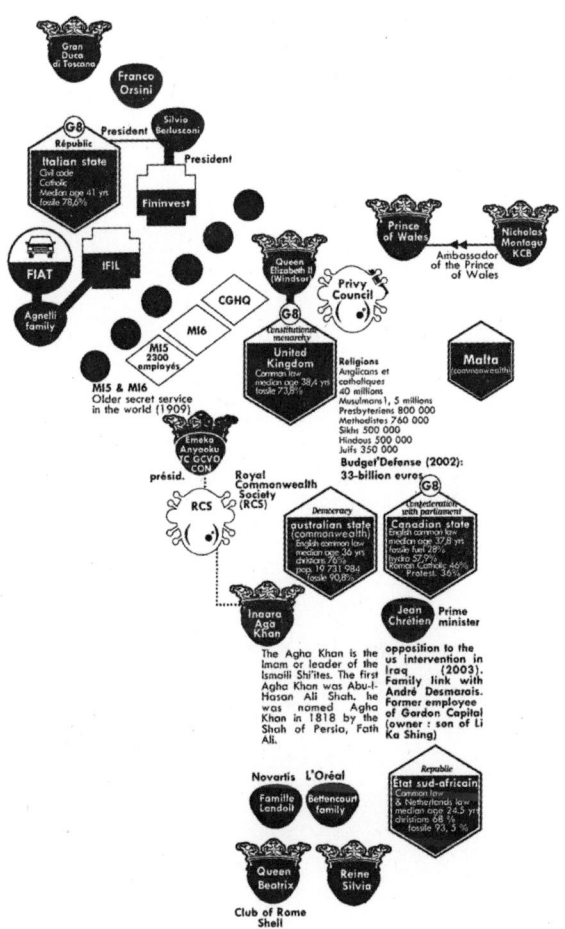

Detail from fig. 15

PART III.
LOOKING FOR PATTERNS: CONSPIRATORIAL DESIGN

A. STYLES AND ROLES
B. A TAXONOMY
C. ESOTERIC TRADITIONS

A.
STYLES AND ROLES

In the previously mentioned essay *The Paranoid Style in American Politics*, historian Richard Hofstadter describes conspiracy theories not simply as a belief or a mentality but as a style. The framework of the style allows for a more nuanced understanding of the issue that goes beyond a simple set of beliefs, including the psychological disposition and the particular rhetorical flourish. For this reason, earlier I referred to conspiratorial design as a style: I consider it an expression of the paranoid style. As we saw at the beginning, Hofstadter compared the paranoid style to an artistic current. Following his comparison let's try to imagine conspiratorial design as a new current in the design field, and let's take a look at what are the aesthetic and rhetorical features that can help us identify it.

OBSCURED KNOWLEDGE → Conspiratorial design is recognizable by a taste for displayed complexity, where a central goal of an artifact is to exhibit extreme convolution, multiplicity, and interconnectedness, without necessarily trying to disclose it. Something similar is described by Manuel Lima in his book *Visual Complexity*[29] as "networkism", the recent infatuation of artists with complex network structures. Some examples of networkism can be seen in works such as Archie Moore's *Kith and Kin* or the work of Thomas Saraceno. When in front of such works the audience often feels like they are in the

---

29 Manuel Lima, *Visual Complexity: Mapping Patterns of Information*, 2011.

presence of a sort of sacred geometry, a work that conceals a well-engineered mystery like an esoteric artifact. Anyone interested in contemporary design might have noticed how a vague taste for esoterism permeates the field. Many young designers seem to be echoing the invitations to re-enchantment[30] present in the philosophical discourse (I'm thinking of authors like Federico Campagna), by repurposing myths, magic traditions, and more or less ancient symbols to represent contemporary issues. I see these kinds of works as part of a broader phenomenon: the diffusion of what I'd call an "aesthetic of obscured knowledge", where a work gestures toward a hidden system, a contemporary condition, or a power structure, yet never fully reveals it—as if veiled by the very complexity it attempts to represent. The subject is there, but it remains slightly blurry, as if it were the viewer's task to complete the image and recognize the shape within the shadow. This "shadow" becomes the aesthetic object itself. There are cases of graphic artists and designers who integrate esoteric symbolism in their works, like Paul Laffoely, Jonathan Barnbrook and the previously mentioned Suzanne Treister, and in some cases even historicized design figures like Victor Papanek. Yet beyond direct references, I believe a more generalized esoteric tone permeates many design practices, partly due to how design is perceived. A design exhibition may appear mysterious to outsiders not

---

30   Marco Mattei, *Invito al Reincantamento*, L'Indiscreto, 2024.

just because they're unfamiliar with the field, but also by curatorial intention. Designers who think of their work as magical also want it to look magical.

INVESTIGATIONS → A frequent trope that design shares with conspiracy theories is the theme of the investigation. It became a standard to define what a design project does (supposedly) rather than what it is, and typically, among the actions that designers say their projects do, they often "investigate". In some cases this rethoric choice comes from an ambition to do what, for example, Forensic Architecture does, namely working for a collective good and fighting injustice (in their case by conducting actual forensic investigations) using the tools of design. But in the case of many design projects, the idea of the investigation and the term "investigate" itself is adopted metaphorically, often in the abstracts, to express what the research that inspired the project was about. The theme of the investigation is then evoked in exhibitions by displaying unintelligible sketches, fragmented atlases of images, and piles of books with bookmarks, to suggest to the spectator that the project itself is just the tip of an abyssal iceberg. By describing this practice I don't mean to dismiss the value of some important research and inquiries that can be made by designers. Rather I want to suggest that adopting this kind of rhetorical tool can be a way to delude ourselves into the fact that a project is truly capable of achieving what it claims, misleading us from other possible means to really achieve those goals.

RPG → As I said, I think the conspiratorial style resides in the visuality as much as in the rhetorics. For example, an important feature of conspiratorial design resides in the rhetorics of the roles. The way designers think and present their role in society, as well as the way they treat and present the information they're asked to process, underlies again an esoteric approach. To explain what I mean by this, let's first take a look at how esoterism is embedded in conspiracy theories.

As the amount of knowledge necessary to understand contemporary society increases and becomes more specific (especially the technical/scientific), access to it becomes a privilege reserved for a few initiates: those who have the time and the resources to engage with the specificity. As a consequence, some people will perceive that information as occult (more or less literally) and treat it as such. And occult information needs a figure who can access the "higher", hidden knowledge and disclose it. This happened with QAnon, where an anonymous user (most probably more than one), signed as Q, convinced many people on 4chan that they were in possession of pieces of information about the secret world order and started to disseminate them with vague hints—the so-called "crumbles" or "Q drops".[31] But as I tried to explain in the previous chapter, conspiracy theories are fundamentally a collective, bottom-up phenomenon: the anonymous user Q may

---

31   Q Alerts. https://qalerts.app/

disseminate the crumbles "vertically", but others are free to embody its role and propose new versions of the theory, as it happens all the time. It is the case of Dylan Louis Monroe, an obscure graphic artist that I consider a prime example of conspiratorial design and the person who designed the diagrams that started my research. Monroe started as a QAnon follower with a background in graphic and fashion design, who in 2017 started producing variations on QAnon theories and formalizing them in huge diagrams (the "deep state mapping project") that went extremely viral—interestingly enough, using an epitome that we could otherwise associate with a designer: "the map-maker". In one of his diagrams (*The Cult of Baal*), Monroe repurposed the "Tree of Life" of Kabalah, an ancient diagram belonging to Jewish mysticism, to illustrate his theories. It's interesting to notice that to illustrate his political ideas he chose a cosmogram. The implicit message was clear: just as the purpose of the Tree of Life was to synthesize esoteric knowledge (the manifestations of God), so his diagram can manage to encompass and evoke a godlike knowledge. Monroe's work was also later exhibited at the Met. The embodiment of the prophetic role is also evident in the archetypes used in the conspiracy discourse. Nobody would like to think of themselves as a conspiracy theorist; it is way more comforting to identify as a heretic, someone who dares to cross the boundaries of the limited conventional knowledge to imagine new worlds. Now, coming back to design, let's consider again this archetype I just described: the revolutionary agitator, who mediates between the people and a higher truth, and that, thanks to the capacity to create new connections, can create a new awareness. It doesn't deviate too much from the archetypical role that many designers identify with and want for themselves. Designers yearn to be wizards: creators of great and abrupt change and innovation, capable of peeking into the future and able to inspire great stupor. As I will try to explain in the chapter "Esoteric traditions", I think this conception has its roots in the origins of design.

RIDDLES AND PROPHECIES → Talking about prophetic figures, I find it meaningful to talk briefly about language and the way I see it used in conspiratorial design. Let's get into the matter of prophecies and riddles. As many design practices and contemporary art become intertwined to the point that it becomes hard to tell them apart, we can witness how many design projects follow contemporary art in its progressive dependency on language. In his *Art School Report*[32] Brad Troemel describes the widespread use of what he calls "artspeak" inside art schools. By "artspeak" he means roughly what Alix Rule and David Levine already defined as "International Art English",[33] namely a mode of expression typical of the art world, whose prime purpose is displaying the belonging to the cultural elite of art (and we can extend that to design as well) and the know-

32 Brad Troemel, *Art School Report*, Patreon, October 2024.
33 Alix Rule and David Levine, *International Art English*, 2018.

ledge of its etiquette, even at the expenses of clear communication. Nonetheless, having a jargon that sounds obscure outside of its field may be partially problematic, but it's also typical of almost every professional field. As Troemel points out, the issue is not that artspeak is not universally comprehensible, but rather that it's not comprehensible by the same people who adopt it. And this happens because clear comprehension is not its goal. The artspeak works by creating a dense cloud of highly sophisticated terms (buzzwords, one may say) whose connections are hard to grasp, inviting in this way the readers to combine them, taking part in a process of collaborative creation of the meaning of the text. Language becomes programmatically ambiguous and open-ended but at the same time exclusive to those who have just enough deciphering tools to participate. This sort of collective game based on allusive riddles is not a social dynamic exclusive to art and design, and I mention it because, once again, I think its peak case study comes from conspiracy theories. QAnon's community engagement was based on collective investigatory games based on the previously mentioned "crumbles". Just to mention some of them, here's a quick selection of the most "information design" ones: *"Information is knowledge, Knowledge is power, Information is power"*-*"Research for yourself"*-*"Focus on the content"*-*"Trust the plan"*-*"Do you see a pattern?"*-*"Learn to read the map"*. QAnon adepts were invited to "learn to read the map", suggesting not to escape from the mysteries but to delve into them to figure them out—or at least have the sensation to have done so. The idea is that the truth is concealed in riddles to keep the profanes out, but the revelation is right behind the corner: you just have to learn the language. At the same time, as Troemel describes, with the rise of conceptual art, art and design schools started implementing assignments for students in the form of riddles—vague and intentionally ambiguous demands that are no longer just a task for the student to perform but a mystery to solve in order to understand what cannot be explained. The assignements are designed with the hope that in the deciphering process, the students will find the truth within themselves and rise as new members of the riddlers. One crucial problem that Troemel points out is that by adopting the artspeak the art community ends up giving up any form of self and reciprocal criticism (in this sense designers adopt the label of "critical" in the same way conspiracy theorists adopt the one of "skeptical"). Esoteric language, both in the case of the artspeak and the "conspiracy-speak" is useful because it's innocuous and can always defuse conflict by shifting the meaning of what everyone intends. In this way, every conspiracy theory and every design project that promises to offer an outlook on possible futures maintains an optimal level of ambiguity and malleability, becoming an always self-fulfilling prophecy; because the prophet never gave a key to it anyway.

B.
A TAXONOMY

After proposing some of the aesthetic and rhetorical features of conspiratorial design, I wish to specify that identifying it is a matter of threshold, and deciding where the threshold sits is a again a matter of ambiguity and intentions. We could think of a sort of taxonomy based on this. We would have three categories: CONSPIRACY BY DESIGN, DESIGN BY CONSPIRACY and CONSPIRATORIAL DESIGN.

CONSPIRACY BY DESIGN would be a very restricted category of works that intentionally recreate or parodize conspiracy theories. Some examples could be the installation *Meme Manifesto* by the collective Clusterduck which recreates the typical conspiracy meme of the 'crazy wall'. The work of visual artist David Dees who creates grotesque images depicting conspiracy theories. Luther Blisset's hoaxes, that in the 1990s were diffusing fake news to then expose bad journalistic practices. The parody religion of Discordianism, that proposes a cult that professes and worships anti-religious concepts like chaos and absurdity. An interesting aspect of this category is connected to the concepts expressed previously about parody mixing with reality. A fascinating case is *Birds aren't real*,[34] a conspiracy theory suggesting that all birds are actually governmental surveillance drones. It was born as a parody of the absurd claims of Trump supporters that ended up

---

34 *Birds Aren't Real*, Wikipedia Foundation. Last edited on 12 March 2025, at 01:19 (UTC).

being inglobated in conspiratorial narratives: thousands of people started believing it, and others who understood its parody nature accused it of being a PSYOP (PSYchological OPeration, i.e. secret govermental acts of mass psychological manipulation) designed to dismiss the value of other valuable conspiracy theories. Even more unsettling is the story of the collective Wu Ming/Luther Blisset who suggest that there are some clues pointing at the fact that whoever started QAnon may have drawn inspiration from their 1999 novel *Q* and from the acts of culture jamming they were operating in that period. In a quote, once again from *Foucault's Pendulum*, that has by now become a kind of modern adage, Umberto Eco captures his concerns about parody with an ironic remark: "Beware of faking: everyone will believe you". I'm not mentioning these cases as a paternalistic warning to "not play with fire," but rather because I find it meaningful to acknowledge that such episodes do exist.

DESIGN BY CONSPIRACY would be the actual conspiracy theories illustrated with design tools. Here the prime example would be the works of Dylan Louis Monroe and his "Deep State Mapping Project", but just as an apex of all the countless vernacular conspiracy diagrams and infographics that you can find online. DESIGN BY CONSPIRACY are works of people who, from outside the world of design, spontaneously understood the rethorics of information design as well its synthesizing and persuasive power, and used it for their purposes.

CONSPIRATORIAL DESIGN

Lastly, CONSPIRATORIAL DESIGN are projects mainly recognized as art or design but that, in the investigative or speculative intentions and in the intricate style, display a conspiratorial aspect. Some examples could be the large-scale infographics of Vladan Joler and Kate Crawford such as *Calculating Empires* or *Anatomy of an AI System*, where they examine the relations between global networks of power and technological systems. Metahaven's *Sunshine Unfinished*—an infographic in the shape of a board game tracing the history of the concept of "transparency" in politics, philosophy, architecture, and other fields. *The Cloud Cosmogram* by Selena Savic, Johannes Bruder, and Maya Indira Ganesh—a speculative diagram about the transformation of human labor within data centers. *The Narrative Structures* of Mark Lombardi—huge diagrams that try to visualize the structures of financial and political power, corruption, and affairs among capitalists, politicians, corporations, and governments. The even more immense diagrams by Bureau d'études, like the ones contained in *Atlas of Agendas*, that with their own style pursue grossly the same attempt as Lombardi. Hans Hackes's *Shapolsky et al. Manhattan Real Estate Holdings, a Real-Time Social System, as of May 1, 1971*, an institutional critique artwork that investigates the exploitative real estate practices in New York City with photographs and diagrams. These are all examples of graphic investigations that, while being all inspiring in their own kind, do not exhaust my definition of conspiratorial design and are not sufficient to express how much I think this style extends. We can perceive the conspiratorial in a lot of contemporary graphic design, for example in some of the work of Boot Boyz Biz, like the publication *Now-Time Issue 1*. Also what I want to argue is that we can find a conspiratorial aspect even in mainstream information design, the one meant for the broad audience, perceived as neutral and informative. With the definition given initially of conspiratorial design, I tried to highlight the tension between the aspiration to encompass a universal scope on a unitary consistent system and at the same time funnel that vision into a persuading synthesis. This same tension can at times appear evidently also in unexpected contexts. An example is *We will be here – Map of the future*, an infographic by Density Design that visualizes the results of a multiplayer online game developed by the Institute for the Future to try to forecast future challenges. Even the data visualizations of Francesco Franchi for Il Sole 24 Ore (the main Italian financial newspaper) display that same "opaqueness" described by Joanna Drucker in the quote mentioned previously that "render invisible the very means through which they function as argument". Data visualizations can create the perception of seeing the world from the control room. Under our eyes in the shape of numbers and graphs, everything in the world falls into place in the same, interconnected, coherent system. Conspiratorial design is ultimately the category of works that try to obtain an illusion of control.[35]

35 *Interview with Florian Cramer | Commentaries: Technology and Policing*, 2025.

Clearly, since this taxonomy is based also on intentions, that are ultimately unknowable, it is destined to remain open. Do some of the mentioned artifacts appear paranoid because their authors are unconsciously paranoid? Hard to tell. Let's take the case of Mark Lombardi as an especially significant one. His work became so compelling in conspiratorial environments also because of some obscure aspects of his personal history. He was found dead in his house hanged by a rope, which was reported as a suicide even if some close to him found it hard to believe he would take his own life. There are some testimonies about some of his works being tampered after his death, which considering the nature of the works can raise the suspicion that someone tried to obfuscate a hypothetical big discovery. Lastly, some of his diagrams were consulted by some FBI agents soon after 9/11 for no specified reason. It's unnecessary to say how much all of these elements fit into a perfect conspiracy theory. However, how we classify Mark Lombardi depends on the lens that we use to see his work. Was he a pioneering critical information designer, an ante litteram schizo-poster, or a saboteur of the state? I think this is open to debate.

After this open-ended attempt to recognize conspiratorial design, I wish to analyze the essential ideas behind it, but only after a quick speculation on how the origins of these ideas can be related to design history.

c.
ESOTERIC TRADITIONS

In the attempt of tracing back some of the seeds of contemporary conspiracism, it could be tempting to identify conspiratorial design just as a recent tendency, a deviation of design from its original noble tension for modernity and rationality. And if on the one hand, I think that the contemporary devaluation of the figure of the designer plays a role, on the other I think it's more relevant to first look back in time and reconsider the idea that rationality is at the core of the discipline of design. In her *Haunted Bauhaus*[36] Elizabeth Otto documents how Bauhaus was far from the image that many have of it as an institution centered around functionality, rationality, and progress. Instead, it was rooted in the ethos of 'Lebensreform', a socio-cultural movement, very widespread in Germany at the time, that criticized the modern industrialized society and advocated for a return to a state of nature through different holistic and spiritualistic practices that included vegetarianism, naturopathy, and gymnastics. It's not too implausible to think that even the notion of 'Gestalt' was so influential inside Bauhaus because it represented a theory of wholeness, very in line with its strive for mystic holism. Bauhaus molded an idea of the designer as a syncretic figure, a mediator, not simply between the industry and the arts, but somehow also between spirit and technique. This theoretical fra-

---

36 Elizabeth Otto, *Haunted Bauhaus: Occult Spirituality, Gender Fluidity, Queer Identities, and Radical Politics*, 2019.

mework is probably what put the basis to the conception, previously mentioned when speaking of design panism, of the designer as someone who deals with *everythingness*, who can see how the parts sum up in a bigger whole. Some of these same ideas that inspired Bauhaus were very influential in the countercultures of the 1960s. Their diffusion was a necessary condition for the birth of ecological ideas that conceive Earth as one big interconnected system. This is also at the base of ideas like Buckminster Fullers "Spaceship Earth' and the *Whole Earth Catalog* by Stewart Brand. In the catalogue of the exhibition *Hippie Modernism: The Struggle for Utopia*, curator Andrew Blauvelt and the other contributors document the influences of figures like Fuller and Papanek in hippie countercultures, who were preoccupied with achieving global social justice and ecological awareness.

> The hippies had a sense of purpose, of making the world anew. Modernism implied that human actions can create a better world, and this demanded an understanding of the whole in which actions take place—better, a critical understanding, which reconsidered the world-changing impact of Industrial capitalism.[37]

Fuller was an interesting example of design's optimistic view towards planetary-scale systems. He was not only convinced that such systems could exist but was actively putting forward the idea that it

37 Andrew Blauvelt, *Hippie Modernism: The Struggle for Utopia*, 2015.

was the role of designers to take care of it. There is a quote in *La speranza progettuale* by Tomás Maldonado that captures Fuller's optimism. There Maldonado writes about the widespread architectural infatuation for megastructures and quotes Fuller as the best example of what he addresses as the "old utopists":

> There can be enough energy and enough organizing capacity so that all men can possess the whole earth.[38]

This idea of a sort of "mega-design" for a "mega-utopia" is the same represented recently in Francis Ford Coppola's *Megalopolis*,[39] where the main character, probably inspired by figures such as Robert Moses, is an almost godly architect who wants to turn New Rome (an alternate version of New York) in a utopia thanks to his ability to innovate and to his genius futuristic vision. With Papanek the idea that design has a responsibility towards society to act ecologically shows also in some of his diagrams, which are all-encompassing descriptions of how society functions as a whole. Much of the appeal of these diagrams comes precisely from the totalizing approach they display. Given the right context, they can appear either as the scribbles of a madman or as the unfolding reflections of an intellectual about society and its almost magical balance (sometimes actually referencing mystical symbols, like the Taijitu). The rise of ecological awareness was also the necessary ground for projects like *The Limits to Growth*,[40]

---

38 Tomás Maldonado, *La speranza progettuale: ambiente e società*, 1971.
39 *Megalopolis*, directed by Francis Ford Coppola, 2024.
40 Donella H. Meadows, Dennis L. Meadows, Jørgen Randers, William W. Behrens III, *The Limits to Growth*, 1972.

a report commissioned by the Club of Rome about exponential growth in a world with finite resources, that in recent times became an obsession of many conspiracy theories who see it as the perfect embodiment of the dreadful globalist elites pursuing a demonic anti-sovereigntism agenda. Some other examples of visual artifacts from that period that anticipated conspiratorial design are *Dow Shalt Not Kill! U.S.A. - Union of Stoned Anarchists* by Sture Johannesson, *I Gerald Ford am the 38th Puppet of the United States* by Emory Douglas and the project of the *Knowledge Box* by Ken Isaacs.

The hippie countercultures of the 1960s were also the cultural humus of alternative epistemologies from which New Age movements emerged, and of which contemporary conspiracy theories are entrenched. The expression 'hippie modernism', coined by Blauvelt suggests a duality that sounds contradictory like the one that I propose with 'conspiratorial design'. A good synthesis of the reason why I find such duality meaningful is expressed in an article by author Tommaso Guariento:

> If we hold fast to the two teachings of the *Corpus Hermeticum*: that there is a Truth in the world, but it is concealed and that man aspires to liberation from his political, social and bodily shackles, we understand how, from the same Hermetic root, identity theories, victimhood and racism and emancipatory revolutionary forces can branch out.[41]

41 Tommaso Guariento, *Critica della ragione cospirativa*, Medium, August 1, 2020

I'm convinced that many aspects of contemporary culture are permeated by this spiritualist esoteric heritage. Not just design, as I briefly tried to suggest, but also many other enviroments, including of course conspiracy theories. We can notice this by observing how conspiracy theories embed various forms of mysticism and occultism, predicating the myth of an ancient epoch of greatness, in contrast to the pursuit, in contemporary society, of control through technology that suppresses our connection with the truth of the universe. We can observe it in the (just apparently) contradictory composition of QAnon followers, who adapted different spiritualist beliefs in a sort of magic conservatism. For example, it's common in these contexts to find people who make traditionalist Christianity coexist with what we can consider as a sort of contemporary Lebensreform. The American alt-right is full of people who are, at the same time, promoting the importance of traditional Christian values to fight the alleged new wave of satanism and explaining how the healing power of crystals is a better alternative to the dangers of modern medicine. The contemporary chaotic cultural wars can be at least partially understood through some core ideas that have recurred throughout history and that were also key passages in the history of design. In other words, I think that, if 1960s utopist countercultures were the heirs of the ideas that inspired Bauhaus, contemporary conspiracy theorists are their deviated grandchildren.

CONSPIRATORIAL DESIGN

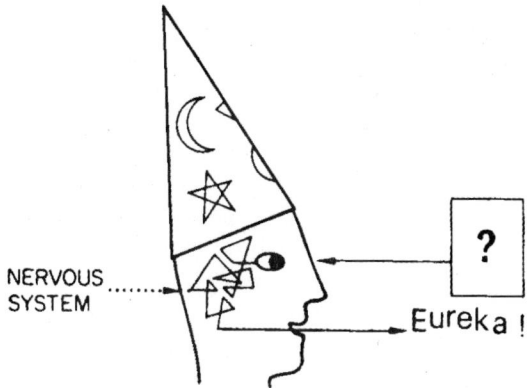

fig. 18   "Designer as a magician" from *Design Methods* by John Chris Jones, 1970.

LOOKING FOR PATTERNS

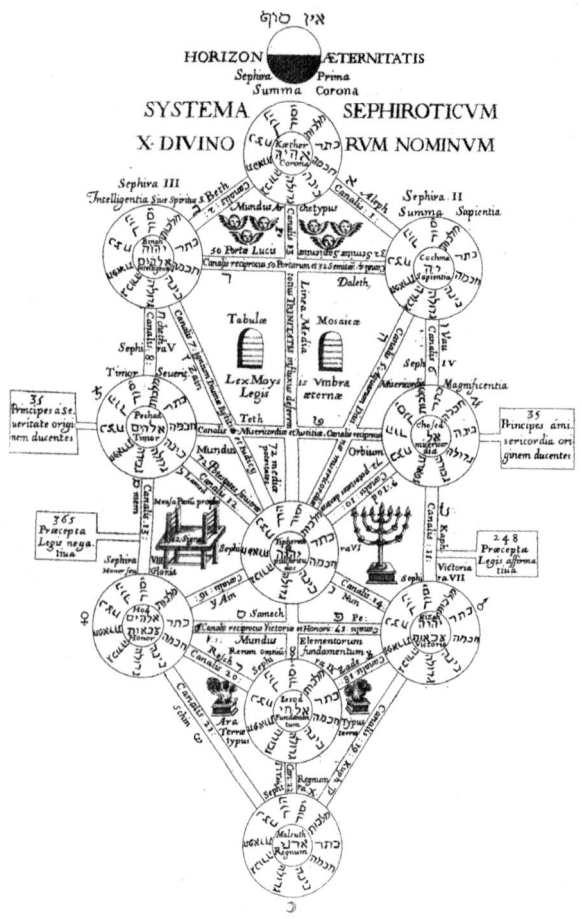

fig. 19   A version of *The Tree of Life* by Athanasius Kircher, published in his *Œdipus Ægyptiacus*, 1652.

CONSPIRATORIAL DESIGN

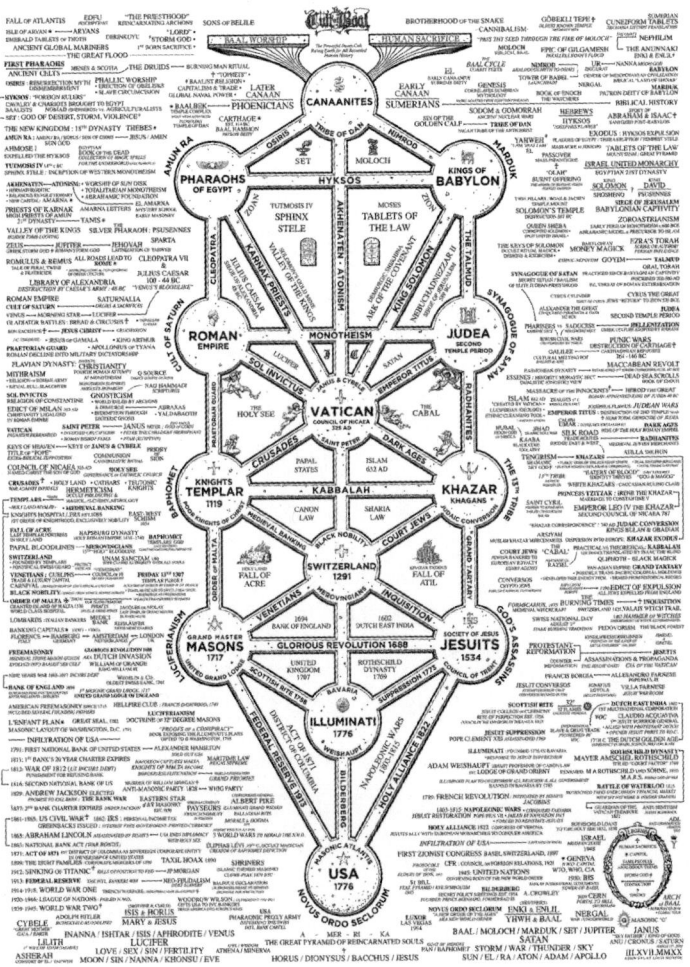

fig. 20   *Cult of Baal*, Dylan Louis Monroe, 2018.
Digital. 8.5 x 11 in. www.deepstatemappingproject.com

LOOKING FOR PATTERNS

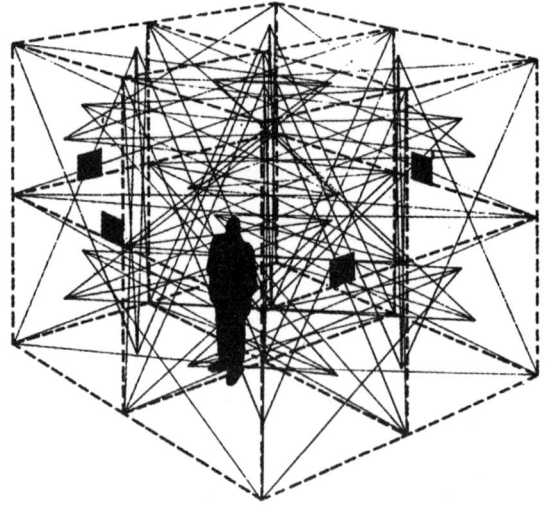

fig. 21   A sketch for *The Knowledge Box*, by Ken Isaacs, 1962. An installation that surrounded viewers with images and sounds, encouraging a more personal approach to learning in a context of information overload.

CONSPIRATORIAL DESIGN

fig. 22   An illustration from Camille Flammarion's *L'atmosphère: météorologie populaire*, 1888. The illustration became a recurring representation of Hermeticism. It appears as a detail in fig. 9

LOOKING FOR PATTERNS

fig. 23   *Dow Shalt Not Kill! U.S.A. - Union of Stoned Anarchists*, Sture Johannesson, 1967.

CONSPIRATORIAL DESIGN

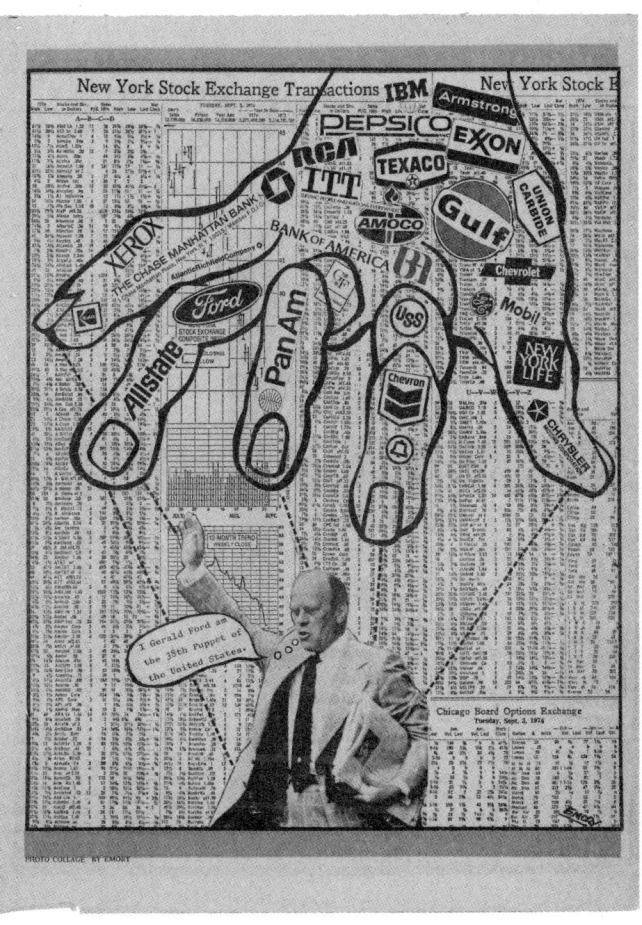

fig. 24 *I Gerald Ford am the 38th Puppet of the United States*, Emory Douglas, 1974.

LOOKING FOR PATTERNS

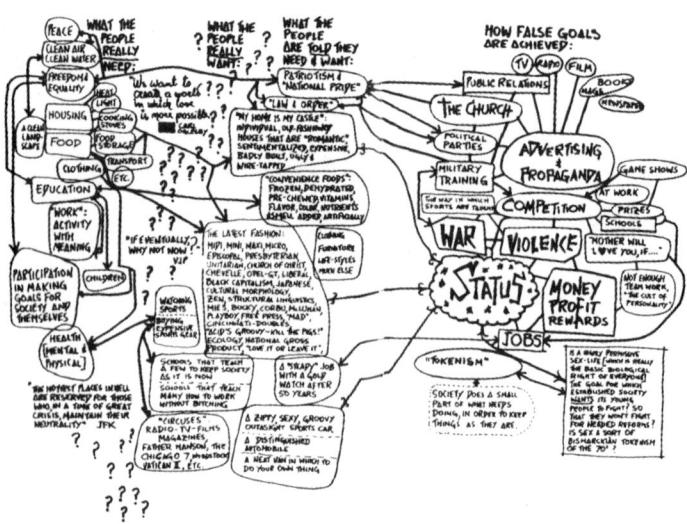

fig. 25   Diagram from *Design for the Real World* (1971) by Victor Papanek.

CONSPIRATORIAL DESIGN

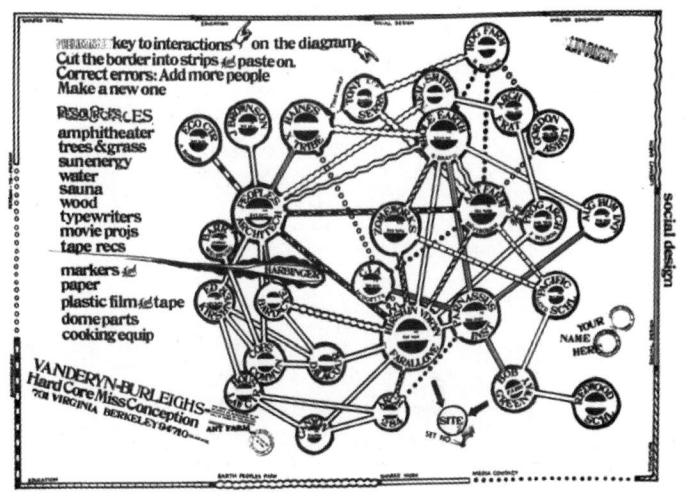

fig. 26   *Freestone Chart* by Curtis Schreirer, 1970.

LOOKING FOR PATTERNS

Detail from fig. 25

CONSPIRATORIAL DESIGN

Detail from fig. 25

LOOKING FOR PATTERNS

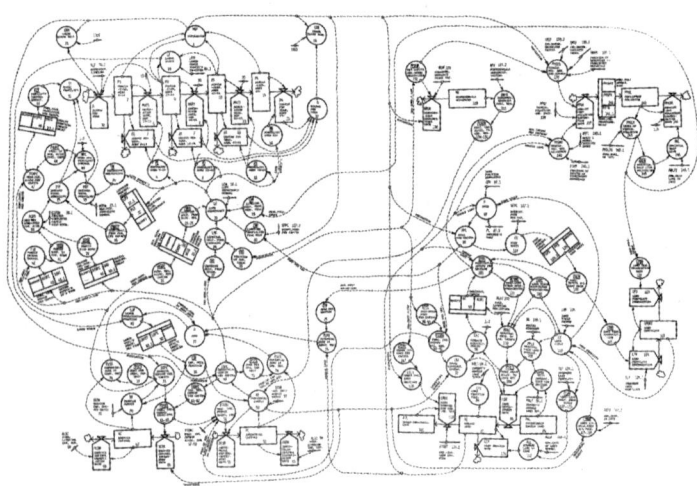

fig. 27   The *World3 Model Diagram*, created by Donella Meadows, Dennis Meadows Jørgen Randers, and William W. Behrens III as part of their work on *The Limits to Growth* (1972). The diagram is the synthesis of a computer model that tries to simulate the interactions between population, industrial growth, food production and limits in earth's ecosystems.

CONSPIRATORIAL DESIGN

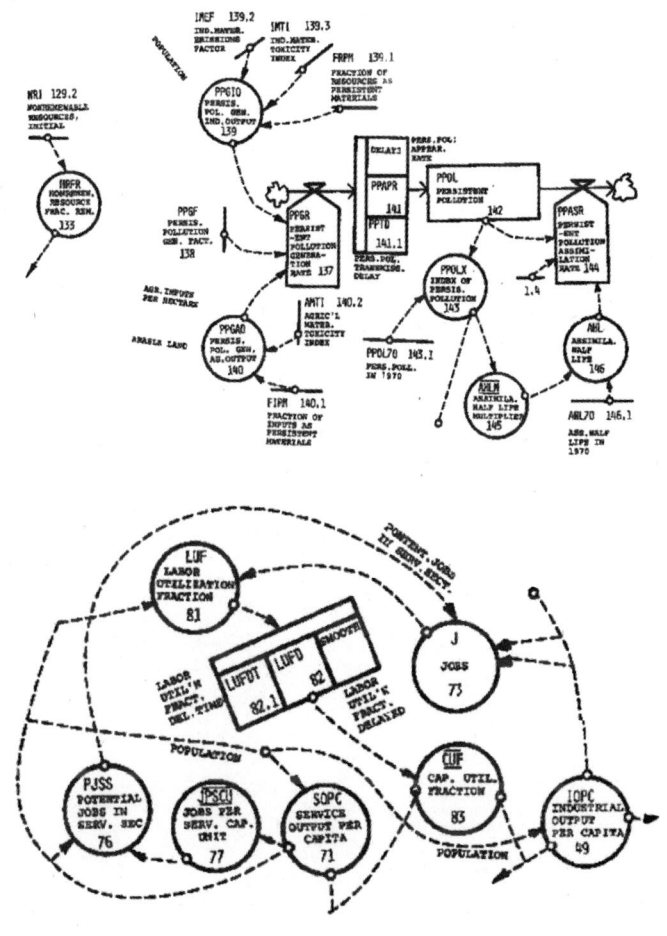

Details from fig. 27

LOOKING FOR PATTERNS

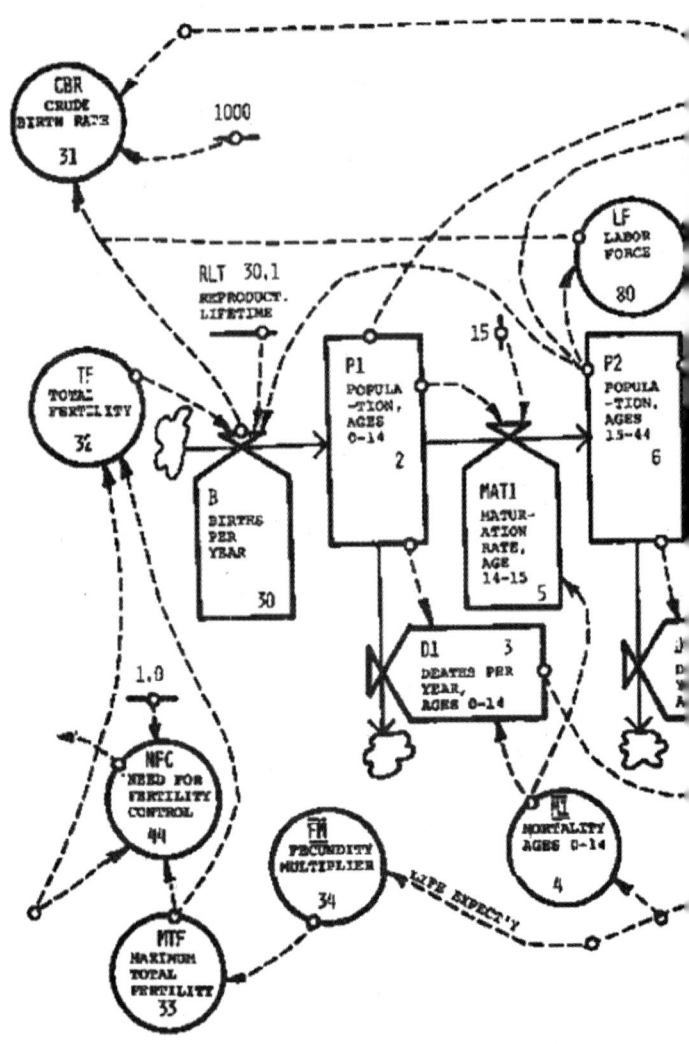

CONSPIRATORIAL DESIGN

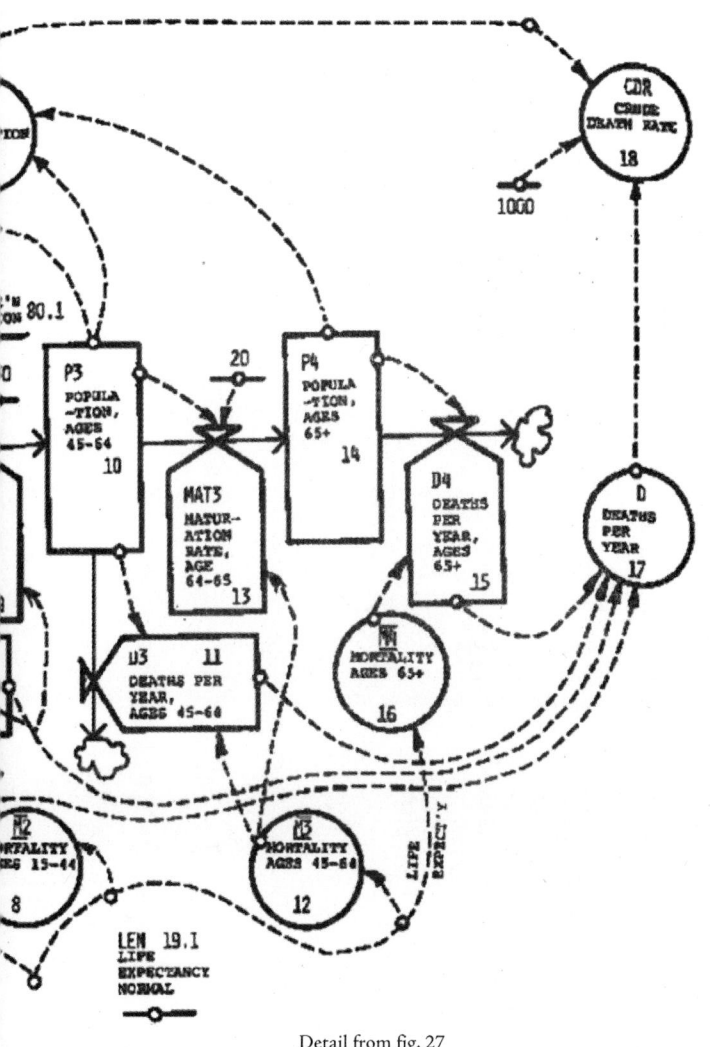

Detail from fig. 27

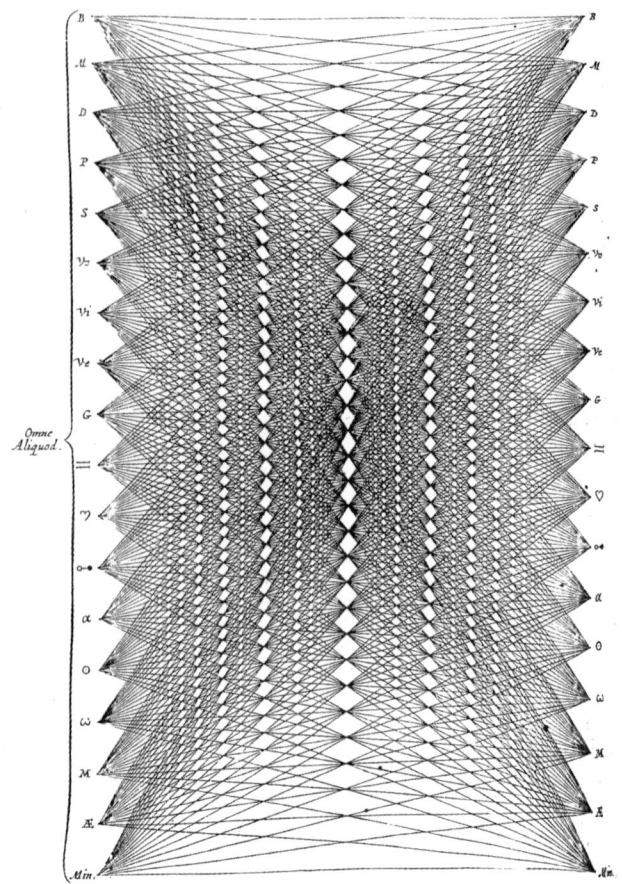

fig. 28 Diagram from *Ars Magna Sciendi Sive Combinatoria* by Athanasius Kircher, 1669. A visual combinatory system of concepts to explore logical relationships and generate new knowledge.

CONSPIRATORIAL DESIGN

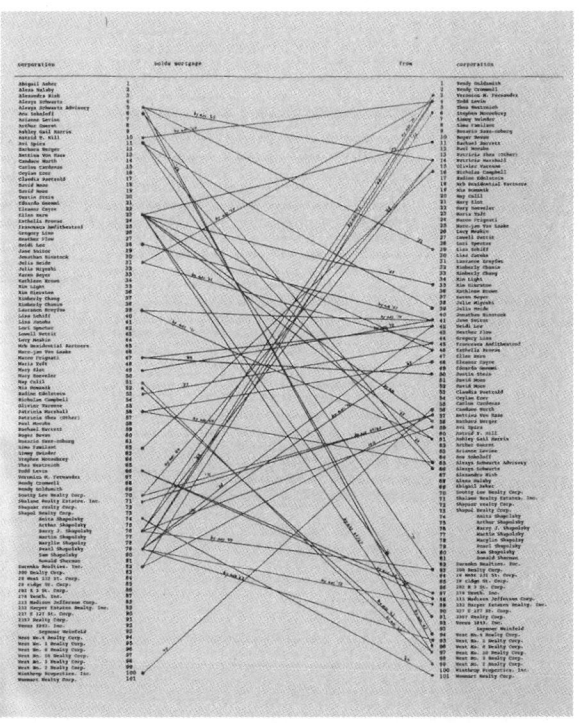

fig. 29 *Shapolsky et al. Manhattan Real Estate Holdings, a Real-Time Social System* (1971), Hans Hacke.

LOOKING FOR PATTERNS

Dispositions: "In Flames"

Disposition

a : prevailing tendency, mood, or inclination

b : temperamental makeup

Two ways of describing humanity's place in the world will coexist throughout the century, one wise and academic, the other wild and interpretative, but which both draw from the same roots, the same questioning that childhood already formulates: who are we, where are we going, where do we come from?

Facteur Cheval

Dispositio

The rhetorical and logical arrangement of matter or discrete elements.

Epicurus modestly hoped that one time or other, a certain fortuitous concourse of all opinions—after perpetual justlings, the sharp with the smooth, the light and the heavy, the round and the square—would, by certain clinamina, unite in the notions of atoms and void, as these did in the originals of all things.

Jonathan Swift, A Tale of a Tub, 1704

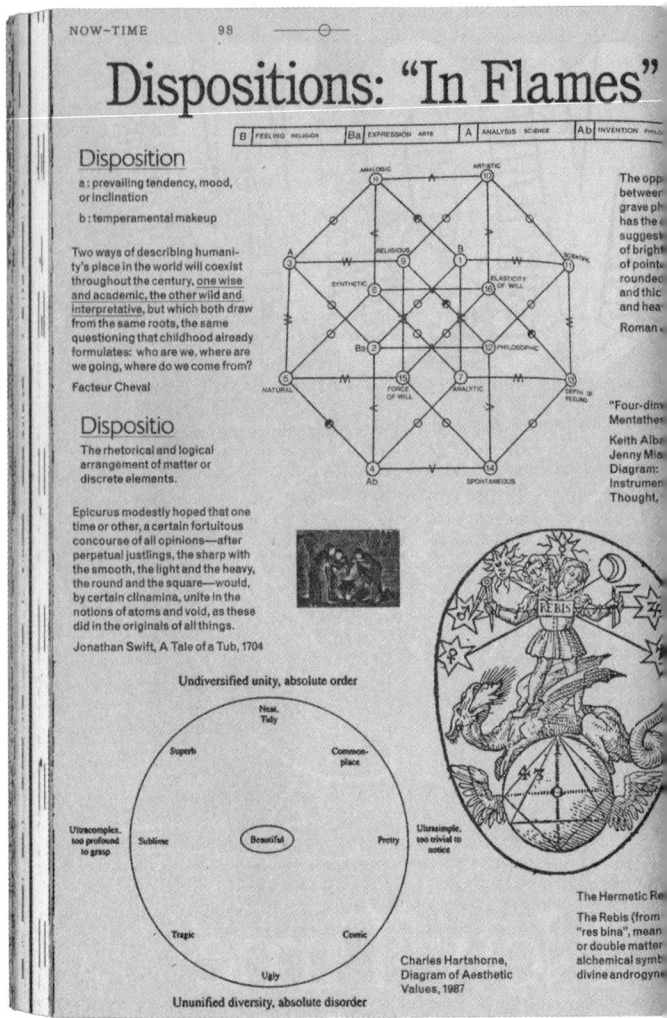

The opp— between grave ph— has the — suggest— of bright— of point— rounded and thic— and hea—

Roman —

"Four-dim— Mentather— Keith Alba— Jenny Mia— Diagram: Instrumen— Thought,

Charles Hartshorne, Diagram of Aesthetic Values, 1987

The Hermetic Re—

The Rebis (from "res bina", mean— or double matter alchemical symb— divine androgyne

CONSPIRATORIAL DESIGN

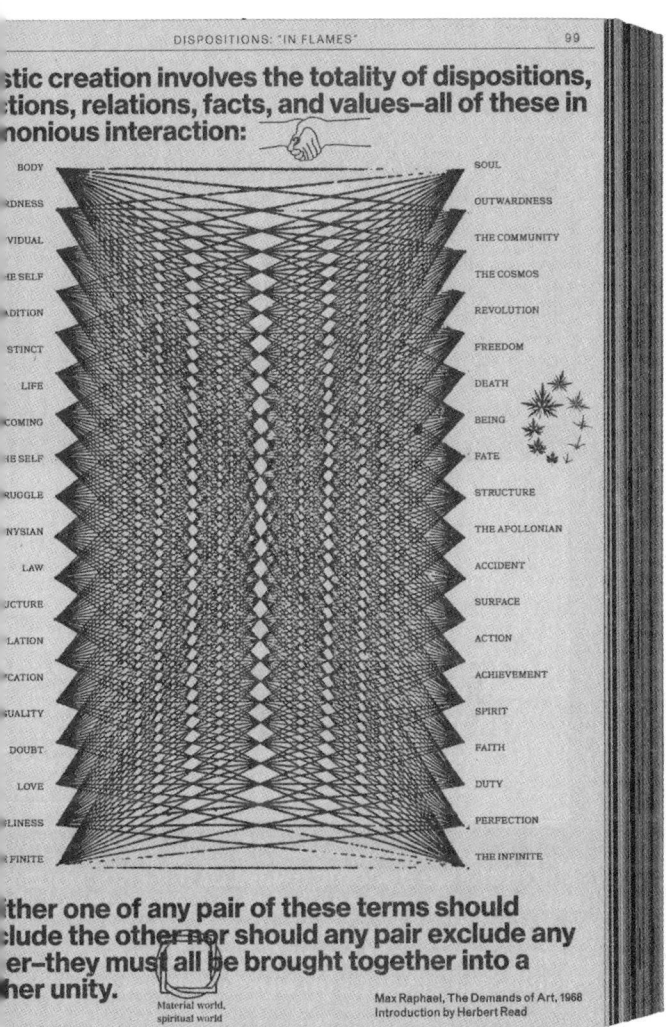

fig. 30   *Now Time Issue 1*, Kevin McCaughey, 2025.

LOOKING FOR PATTERNS

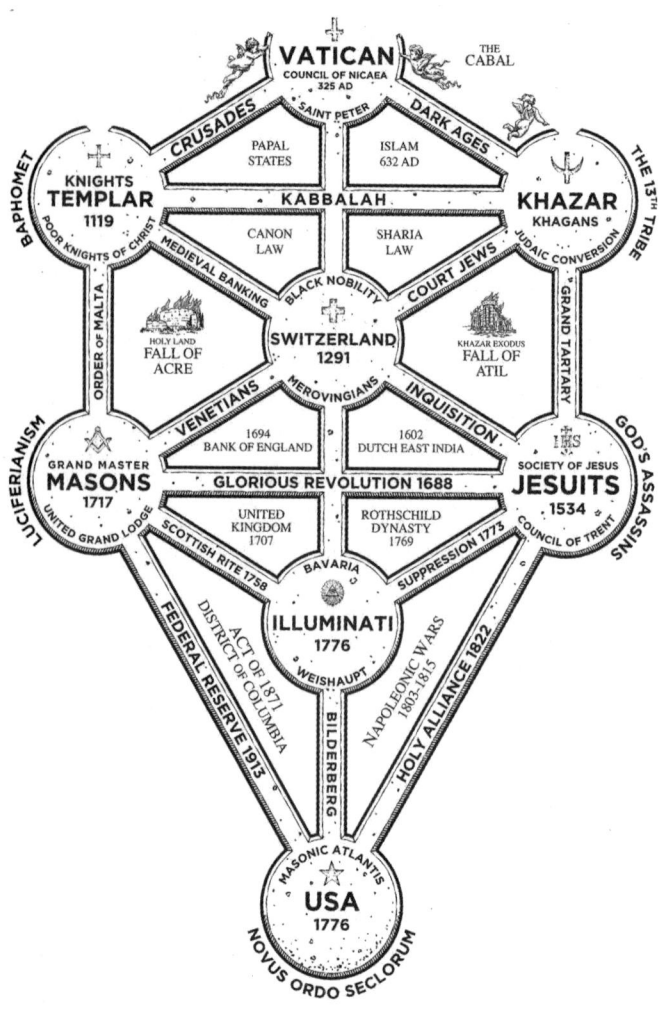

Detail from fig. 20

CONSPIRATORIAL DESIGN

fig. 31 *Beyond the Blue Marble: Summer Camp for Planetary Imaginaries,* by Baltan Laboratories and Chimerical Intelligence Lab. Graphics by Ianis Dobrev and Delphine Lejeune, 2025.

LOOKING FOR PATTERNS

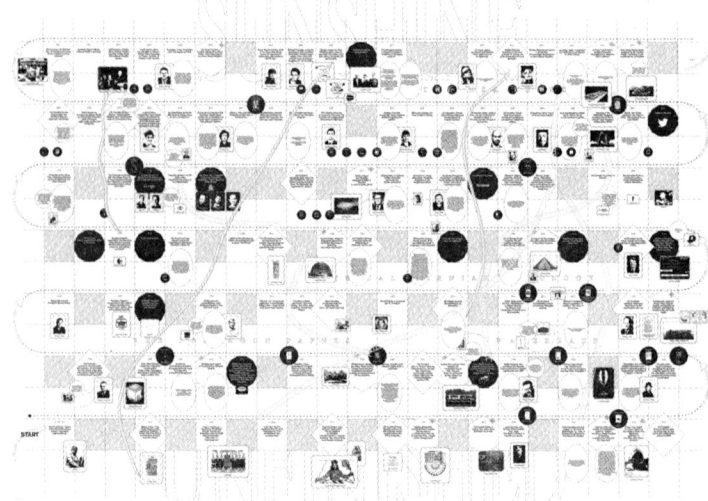

fig. 32 An infographic from the project *Sunshine Unfinished*, by Metahaven, 2015. where they follow the structure of a board game to illustrate the history of the concept of "transparency" in various contexts, from the Roman Empire to Wikileaks.

CONSPIRATORIAL DESIGN

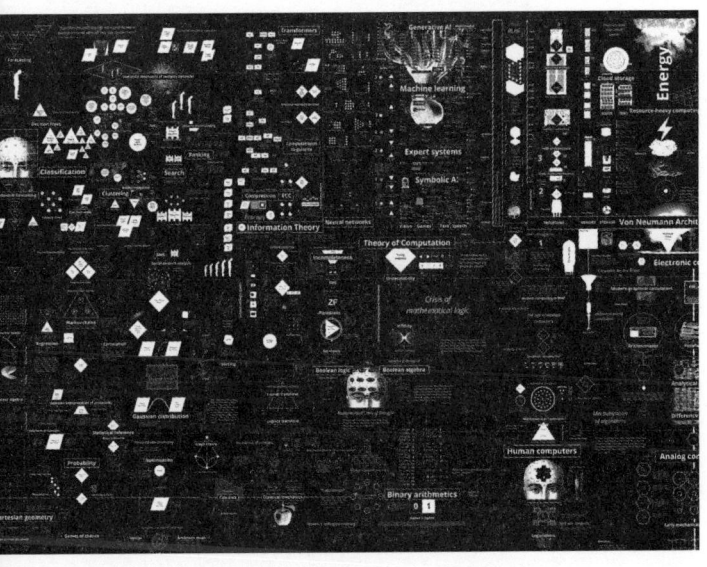

fig. 33 A section of *Calculating Empires*, Kate Crawford and Vladan Joler, 2023. A large scale infographic that tries to show patterns of colonialism, militarization, automation, and enclosure since 1500.

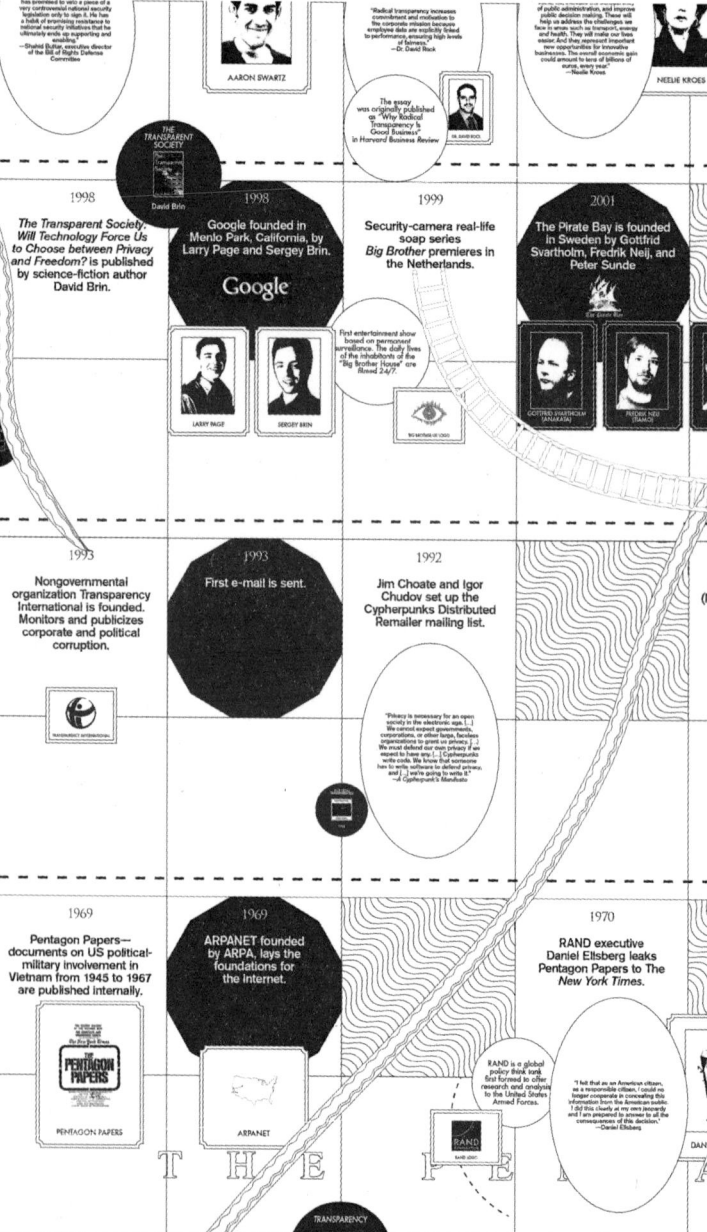

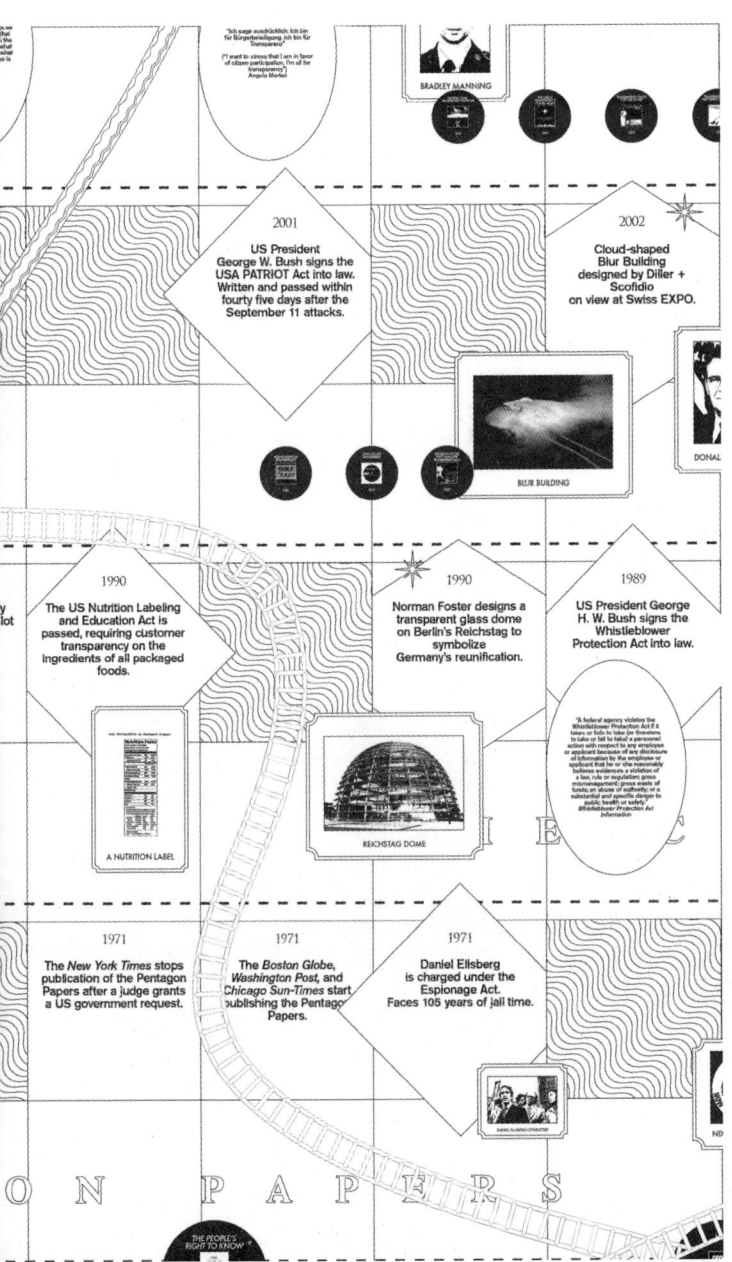

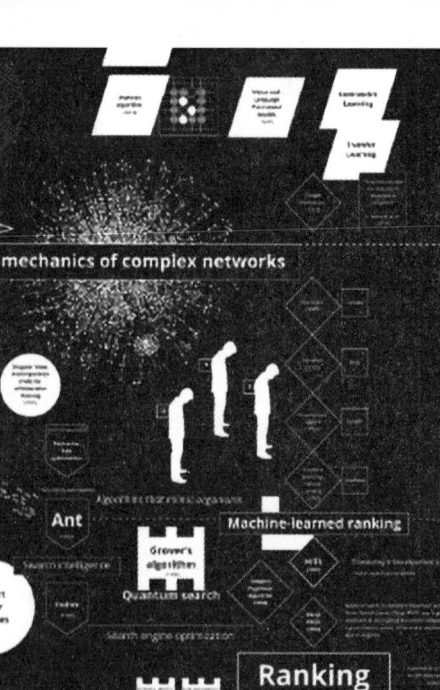

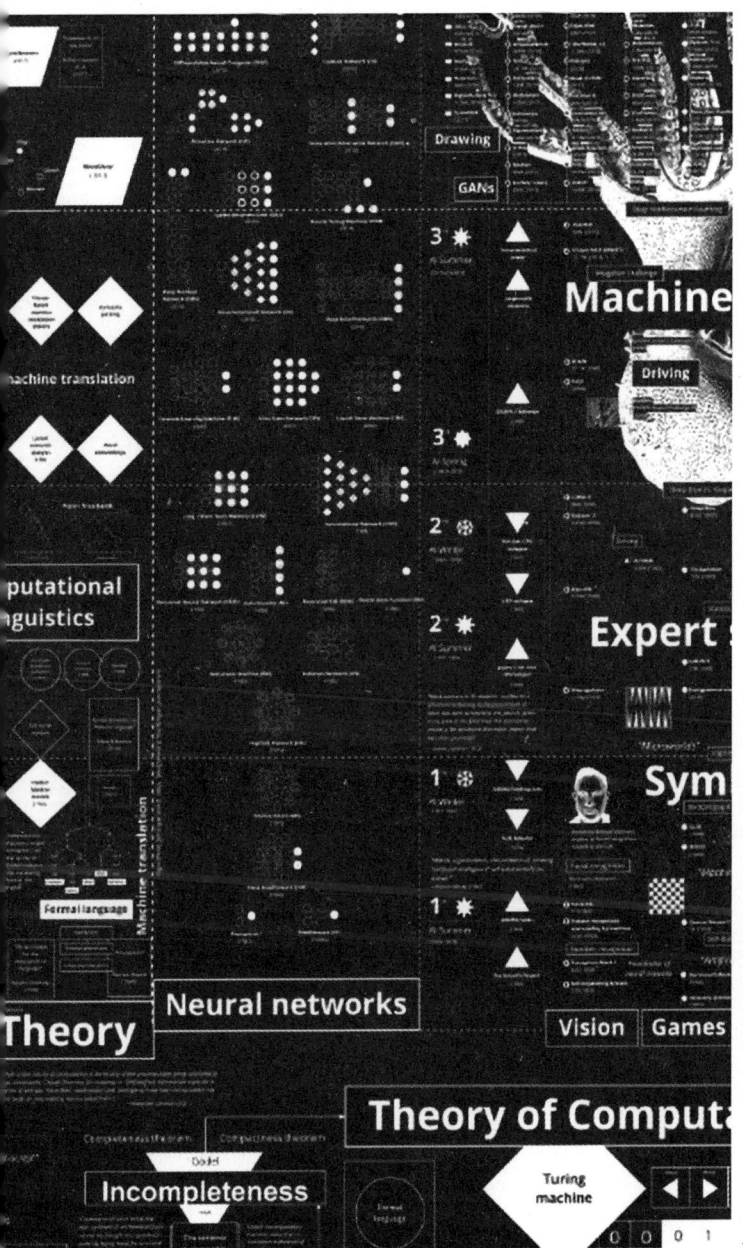

LOOKING FOR PATTERNS

fig. 34   *We will be here – Map of the future*, Density Design, 2008.

CONSPIRATORIAL DESIGN

fig. 35   *Cloud Cosmogram*, Selena Savic, Johannes Bruder and Maya Indira Ganesh, 2019.

LOOKING FOR PATTERNS

Detail from fig. 34

CONSPIRATORIAL DESIGN

Detail from fig. 35

PART IV.
SEEING IT ALL: THE BIGGER PICTURE

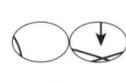

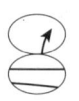
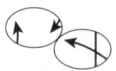

A. CONFIRMATIONS ONLY
B. THE BIGGER PICTURE

A.
CONFIRMATIONS-ONLY

As mentioned earlier when talking about networkism, conspiratorial design is bound to the use of complexity as an aesthetical and rhetorical tool. This shows evidently in its obsession with size: the size of the theory and consequently the size of its visualizations. Let's take once again Dylan Louis Monroe. His most successful diagram, the Q-Web, is an enormous hyper-intricate diagram that tries to show an alleged hidden history of humanity. To most viewers, the visual features of the Q-Web would immediately reveal its fallacies. Just by quickly observing the insane amount of connections and noticing the immense attempted explanatory scope, one could understand how it involuntarily visualizes all the biases underlying the thinking process, as well as the general paranoid style behind the whole theory. It is so extremely complicated that it aroused a sense of surprise and often of ridicule in the people I showed it to when I first started this project. Recently the term "schizoposting" emerged in meme culture to refer to this kind of content. Briefly, schizoposting means producing content (mainly with a parodistic intent, but not necessarily) that recreates the disconnected rants of someone with paranoid schizophrenic disorders. The idea of producing artworks by drawing inspiration from a state of self-induced paranoia has its noble precursors in visual arts, like the "paranoiac-critical method" by Salvador Dalì. In the context of conspiratorial design I think it's secondary to understand wether or not the nodes of the diagram are fake information, while it's more relevant to notice how the connections between them are vague and equivocal. At times they try to show consequentiality, at other times similarity, and in many cases, it's not even clear why one point is connected to another at all. If one would want to mock the Q-Web one would probably use the 'Charlie Conspiracy' meme from *It's Always Sunny in Philadelphia* with the classic image of the 'crazy wall'. The 'crazy wall' is the recurring image present in pieces of detective fiction where the obsessive inconclusive investigation is carried out by pinpointing interconnected pieces of evidence on a board. But if recognizing the Q-Web as a crazy wall comes easy for many, it didn't for many others, who in 2018—when the Q-Web went viral—were strongly persuaded of the quality of Monroe's ideas, also thanks to his visualization effort. Of course, criticizing it for its lack of rigor is dutiful, but the Q-Web is not dissimilar to other forms of visual inquiry in its method. Displaying a cloud of available information and trying to make your pattern-recognition mechanisms look for meaning in it is something we do all the time, especially in design. It's a common practice for designers, both in the research and presentation phase, to work with mood boards, in which the information gets cherry-picked and arbitrarily connected to make a convincing message emerge. Like in the "starter pack" meme format—where to make fun of a stereotype one clusters some elements that identify it—the trick is that if you manage to nail two or three key elements that clearly suggest what you want to evoke, you will create a mental framework for everybody else to collocate the other elements in it. Not all of the elements need to be as strongly meaningful to still contribute by accumulation to the general meaning. The fact that intuitive inquiries by visual association are not fully rigorous doesn't mean they cannot be helpful in making meaningful patterns emerge. One could argue that even John Snow's 1854 famous map of cholera—often rightfully presented as an early example of information design's inquiring potential—proceeded similarly, and yet it saved lives. The issue lies rather in the discrepancy between the intuition-based inquiry and the ambiguity in the message that results from the accumulation of elements. As Claire Bishops explains in her article *Information Overload*,[42] size often acts as a rhetorical tool in research-based artworks, when the audience gets overloaded with an amount of research that is basically impossible to respond to. This brings us back to the expression used initially, in the definition of conspiratorial design as a 'hypertrophic synthesis'. What I mean by hypertrophic synthesis is the kind of paradox that the diagrams in this book present, where a tension to be all-encompassing produces the impression of a synthesis. But this synthesis to sustain itself always needs to grow to a larger scale. Conspiratorial diagrams never 'prove' anything, they just postpone the conclusions with another possible connection. Like a conceptual version of a tensegrity structure by Buckminster Fuller, which instead of being self-sustaining, needs to keep expanding to not collapse. The consequence of develo-

---

[42] Claire Bishop, *Information Overload*, Artforum, September 21, 2023.

ping research inside a system that expects only confirmations is that one will always manage to create new connections, to expand the theory by building upon it. Umberto Eco in *The Limits of Interpretation*[43] referred to uncontrolled interpretation as a "cancer" growing constantly, unable to cut out the excess. The metaphor is sharp but it expresses well the problematic aspect of this approach to knowledge creation: the interpreters can associate an exponentially growing number of meanings as every new sign is added to the cloud until they are convinced, and try to convince others, that the quality of the interpretation is proven by its size.

In conspiratorial design, design and conspiracy theories share not only the same methods and tools for representation but also the same persuasion stratagems, which are now used in circumstances they were never meant to be. Conspiracy theories are design's Frankenstein monster and studying them must push us to acknowledge the responsibility that should follow from the cohesive ability and persuasive power of design.

B.
THE BIGGER PICTURE

Throughout this book, I tried to focus on the blurry borders of design and conspiracy theories. The last aspect I wish to tackle is the main root of conspiratorial design where all the other stylistic aspects have origin. Conspiracy theories and design tend to understand the world with large-scale systems, often ending

---

43 Umberto Eco, *The Limits of Interpretation*, 1990.

up with creating a totalizing doctrine. But I think this should not be interpreted as a form of naiveté. Even though we might find the hyperconnected visions of world-plans proposed by conspiracy theories to be paranoid and even ridiculous, I think they conceal a basic human necessity that we must take very seriously: the need for order. The need to have faith in an ordered vision that gives meaning to the otherwise fragmented and and tragic events of a hard-to-swallow reality. To fulfill this purpose, such a vision has to act as a framework capable of inglobating the totality of the episodes, signs, and symbols surrounding us. As designers, we are constantly asked to synthesize complex matters we are not experts in, into outputs that make them graspable by other non-experts. But what happens when the complex subject is too complex? When it is, in fact, a totality? Resorting once again to Jameson's concept of cognitive mapping as our ability to understand and navigate complex social and spatial relationships, and using his interpretation of conspiracy theories as a form of people's cognitive mapping of an ungraspable totality, we could conciliate the design's and the conspiratorial's quest for a *bigger picture*. What I mean by 'bigger picture' is the typical conspiratorial trope according to which there is a truth that can be seen if you can look at the evidence from the right point of view—if only you take a step back. In detective stories the bigger picture is the moment in which the sense of vague apophenia emanated by the crazy wall finally discloses itself to the detective, revealing the pattern. But in our case the bigger picture is also literally a picture: an image that can synthesize a whole and evoke it instantaneously in the viewer's eye. This profound faith in the ability of images to achieve this purpose was picked up by conspiracy theories but was theorized and formalized by designers in the first place. In his book *L'ordre Compliqué* Yona Friedman writes about the creation of images as a fundamental practice in the architecture-based cosmology he describes.

> Words are perfect for analyzing an experience; to express totality, we need images. To construct an image - this, then, is the basic contradiction. To construct: that is, to put elementary things together, and form from them a unitary thing. The image, on the other hand, is from the outset a unitary thing, which loses all value if you break it down. I do not know reality, but it seems to me that one can only deal with it by means of the image. […] The entire history of mankind can be represented by a sequence of images.[44]

But as suggested earlier, design's quest for the bigger picture, for the act of whole-making, can be traced back at the very roots of graphic design, in the concept of Gestalt.

> Or one sees a series of discontinuous dots upon a homogenous ground, not as the sum of dots, but as figures. Even though there

---

44 Yona Friedman, *L'ordre compliqué: et autres fragments*, 2008.

may have been a greater latitude of possible arrangements the dots usually combine in some spontaneous, natural articulation and any other arrangement even if it can be achieved is artificial and difficult to maintain. When we are presented with a number of stimuli we do not as a rule experience a number of individual things—this one and that. Instead larger holes separated from and related to one another are given an experience. Their arrangement and division are concrete and definite.[45]

Design's role is to produce images, as images express a totality, and the totality *raises awareness*. The concept of "awareness" plays in design the same role that the concept of "awakening" plays in QAnon. According to QAnon, "The Great Awakening" will be the moment in which the population finally sees the bigger picture and acknowledges the great plan, defeating the conspiracy and reaching a state of utopia. In the quest for the bigger picture design has grown in terms of multidisciplinarity, abstraction, and goals. The struggle in trying to create an image of the whole is that to see the image in its totality, so that all the pieces join, one would need to take infinite steps back. Quoting once again Tomás Maldonado in *La Speranza Progettuale*, in a passage about "the old utopists" Maldonado writes:

---

45 Excerpt of Max Wertheimer's *Dot Essay* (1923) from David Reinfurt *A *New* Program for Graphic Design*, 2019.

SEEING IT ALL

Although we recognize, as we have already said, the formidable contribution of innovation and stimulation of these designers, it seems to us that they fail to overcome the contradictions inherent in those who believe in the maieutic power of images and prophetic words alone.[46]

---

46 Tomás Maldonado, *La speranza progettuale: ambiente e società*, 1971.

CONSPIRATORIAL DESIGN

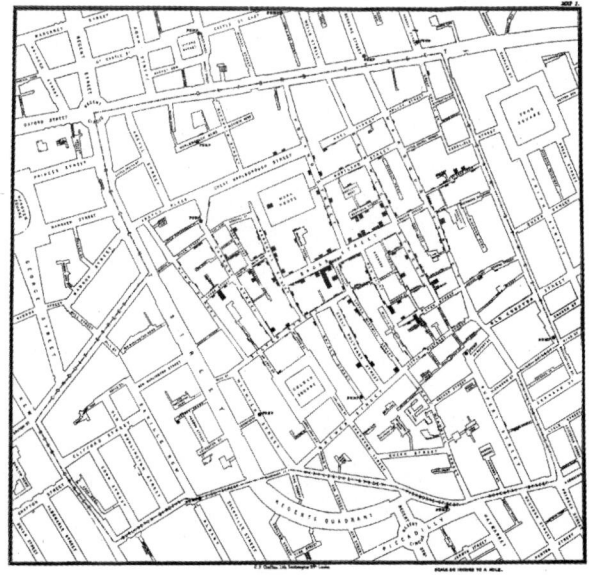

fig. 36   Map by John Snow showing the clusters of cholera cases in the London epidemic of 1854

SEEING IT ALL

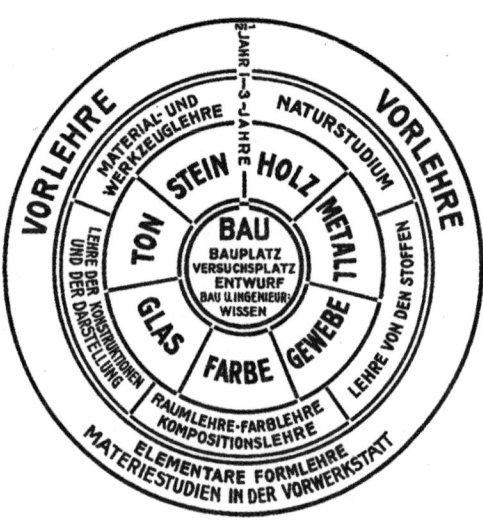

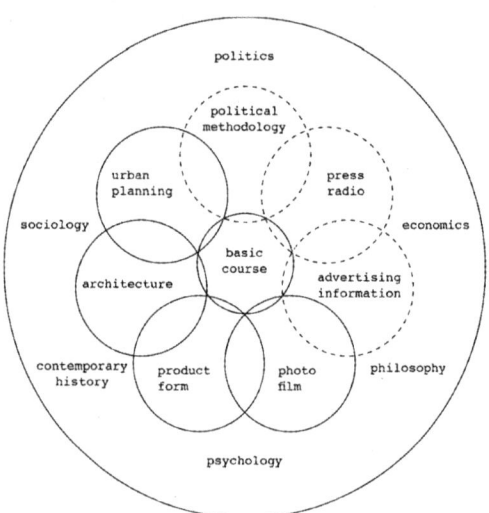

CONSPIRATORIAL DESIGN

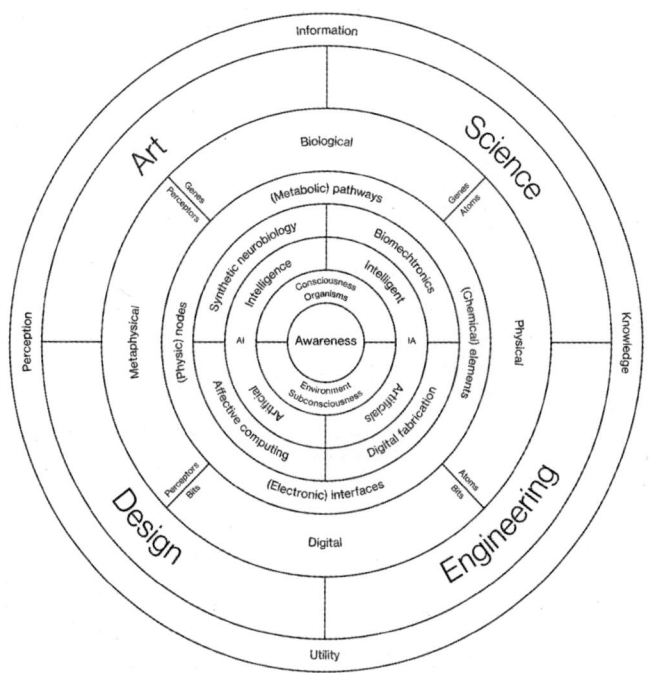

The evolution of a diagram shows how design has broadened its conceptual scope.

fig. 37 Diagram by Walter Gropius—contained in *Idee und Aufbau des staatlichen Bauhauses* (1923)—explains the teaching structure and the subjects at Bauhaus.

fig. 38 Inge Scholl and Otl Aicher do the same for Ulm HFG (1953): this time the subjects are broader and more conceptual.

fig. 39 *The Krebs Cycle of Creativity* diagram by Neri Oxman (2020) illustrates her view about the interaction between disciplines that produce innovation in an all-encompassing diagram—it includes "physical" and "metaphysical" (so, literally, everything) and at the center there is "Awareness".

SEEING IT ALL

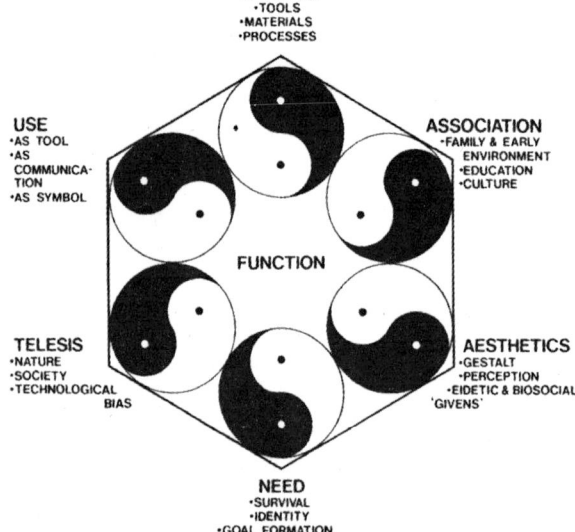

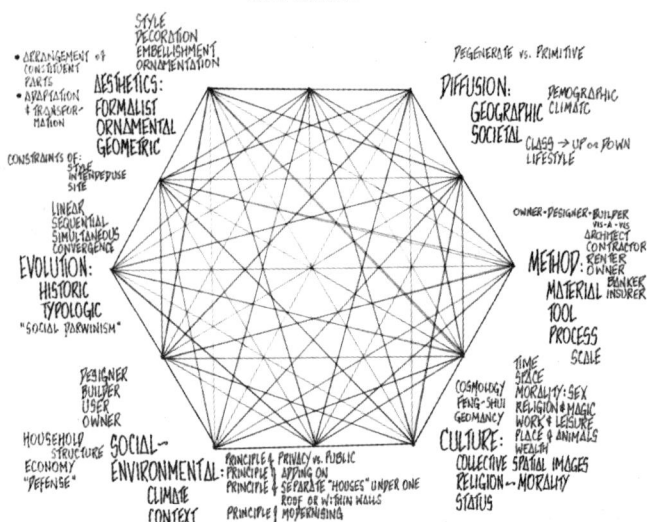

CONSPIRATORIAL DESIGN

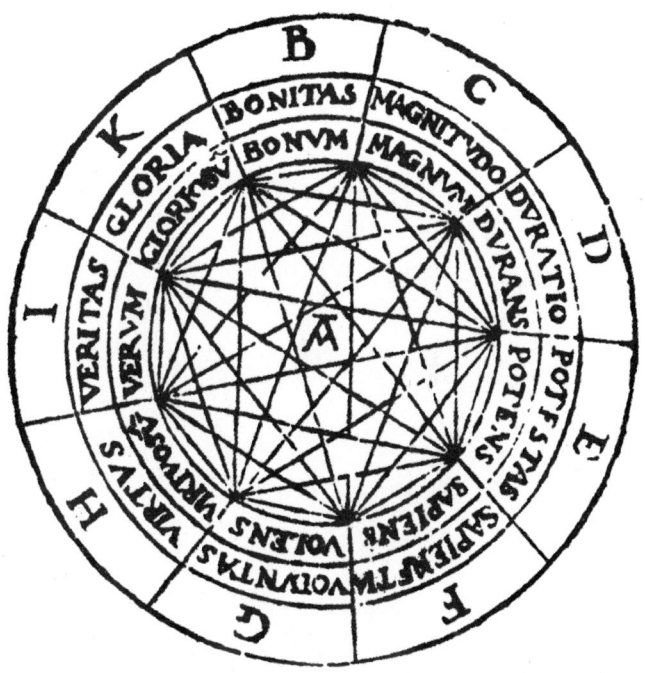

fig. 40-41   Two diagrams by Victor Papanek explaining his conception of design, respectively from *Design for the real world* (1971) and *The Green Imperative* (1995)

fig. 42   A diagram, from *Ars Magna* by Ramon Llull, 1308. A visual and logical device designed to systematically combine fundamental concepts in order to explore all possible relations between them, demonstrate theological and philosophical truths, and provide a universal method of reasoning.

LOOKING FOR PATTERNS

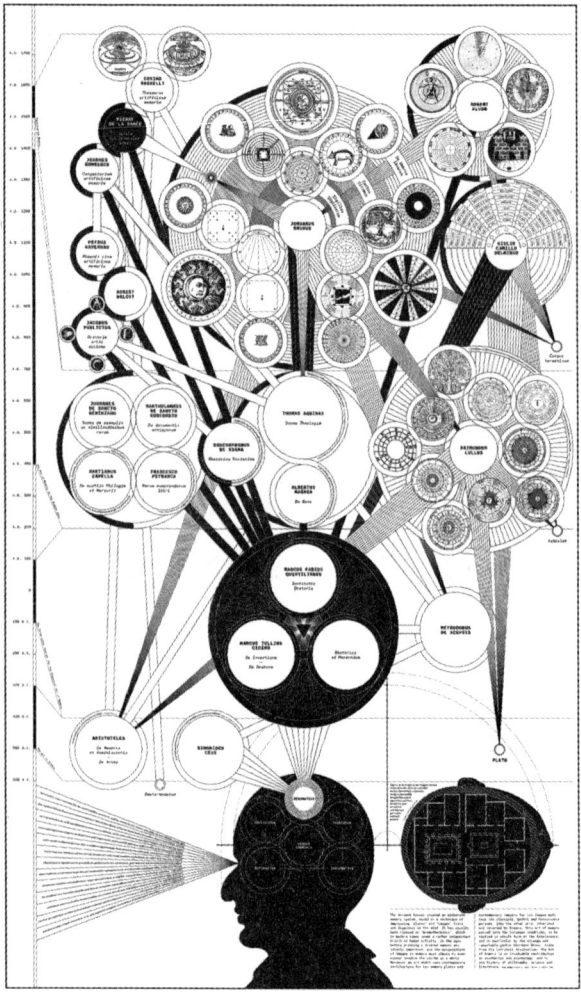

fig. 43   *The Art of Memory* by Francesco Franchi, 2013.
An infographic that illustrates the chronological
development of mnemotechnics.

CONSPIRATORIAL DESIGN

Detail from fig. 43

SEEING IT ALL

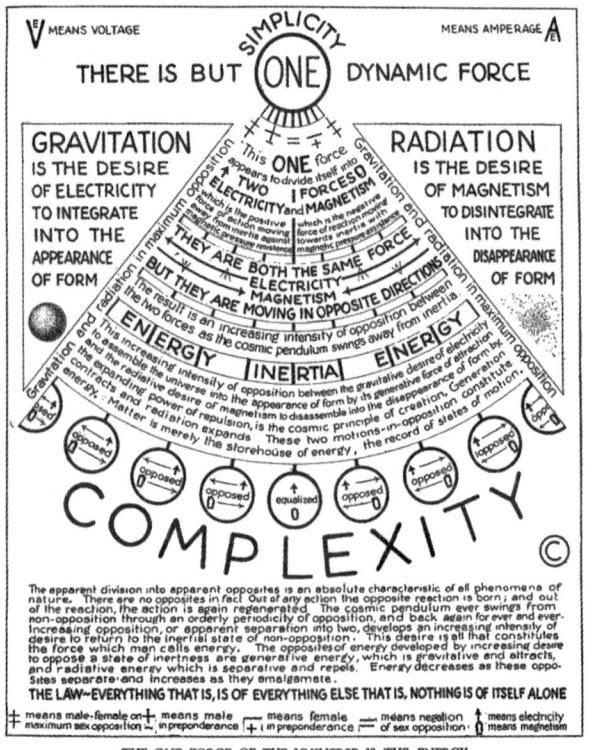

fig. 44   *There is but ONE Dynamic Force*, a diagram by Walter Russell from his book *The Universal One* (1926) that claims to unify all motion, matter, and energy through the pulse of a single divine force.

CONSPIRATORIAL DESIGN

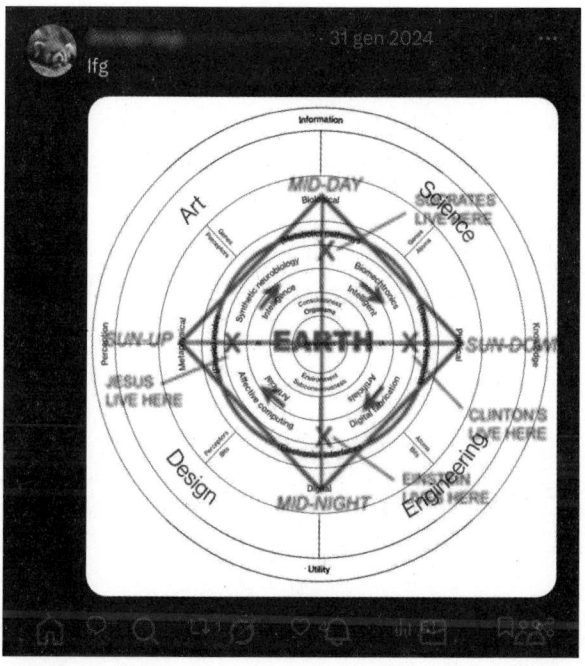

fig. 45   A user on X makes fun of Oxman's *Krebs Cycle of Creativity* diagram by superimposing it on the *Time Cube*, a diagram representing a rambling conspiracy theory that is used in some online niches as a meme to express "abstruse nonsense", 2024.

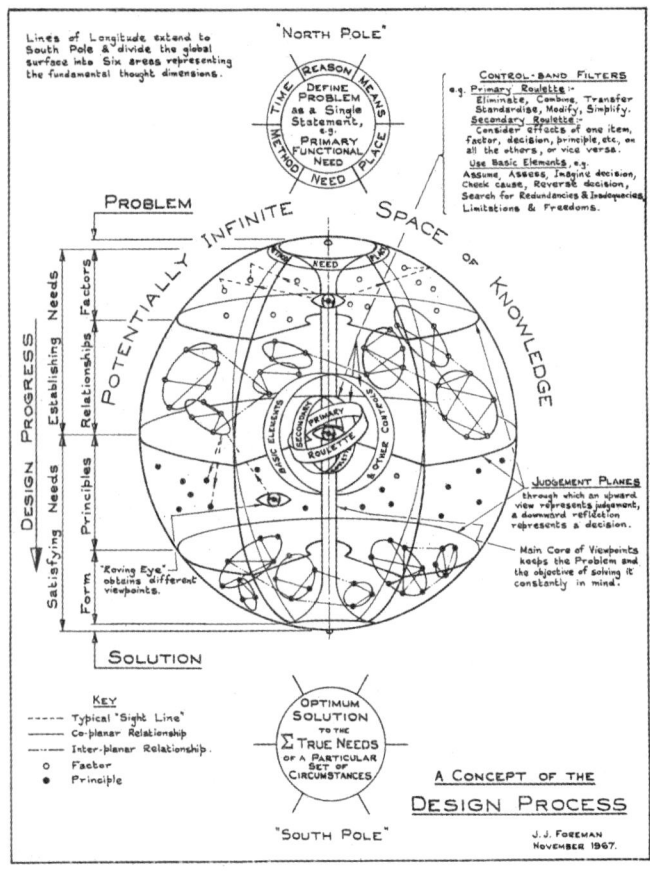

fig. 46 A diagram explaining the design process featured in *Design Methods* by John Chris Jones, 1970.

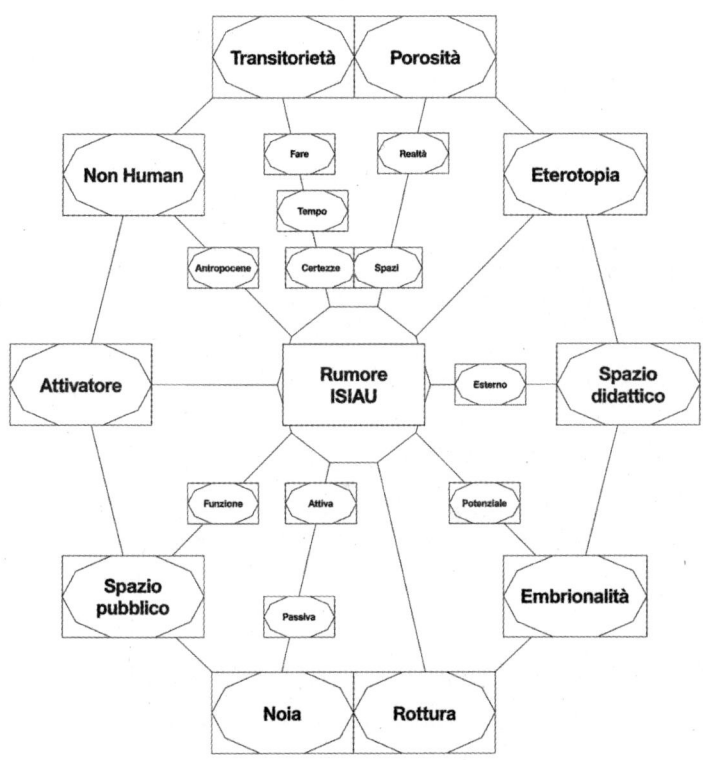

fig. 47　Diagram developped by students of the Editorial Design MA at ISIA U for the course "Methodology of Design", taught by Marco Tortoioli Ricci as a manifesto for the project *Rumore*, 2024.

LOOKING FOR PATTERNS

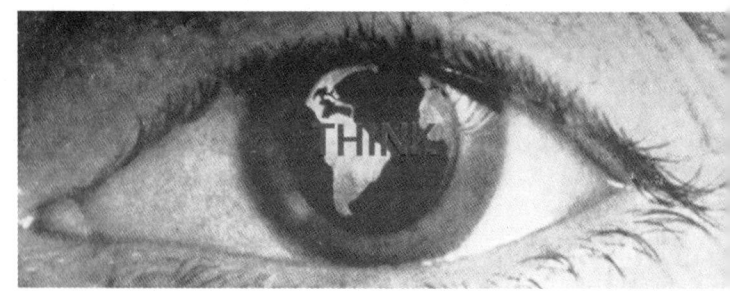

Detail from fig. 23

CONSPIRATORIAL DESIGN

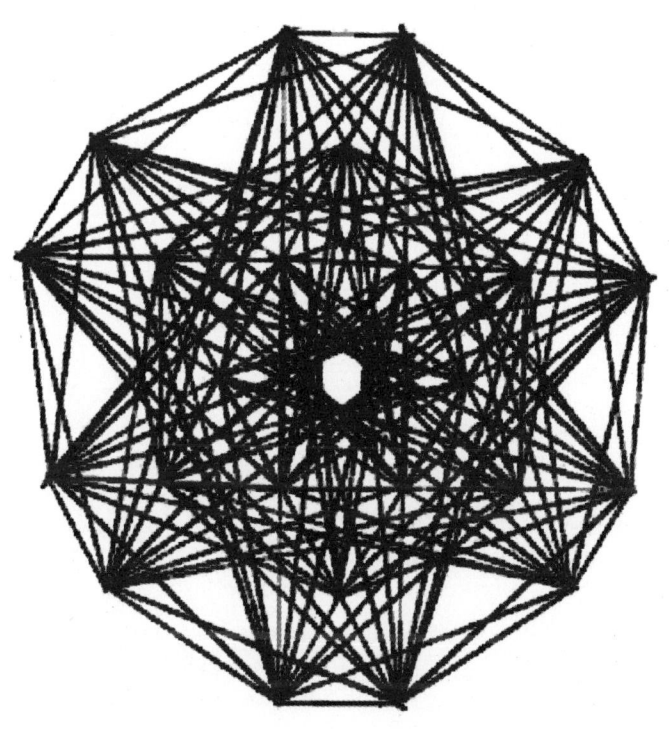

Detail from fig. 11

SEEING IT ALL

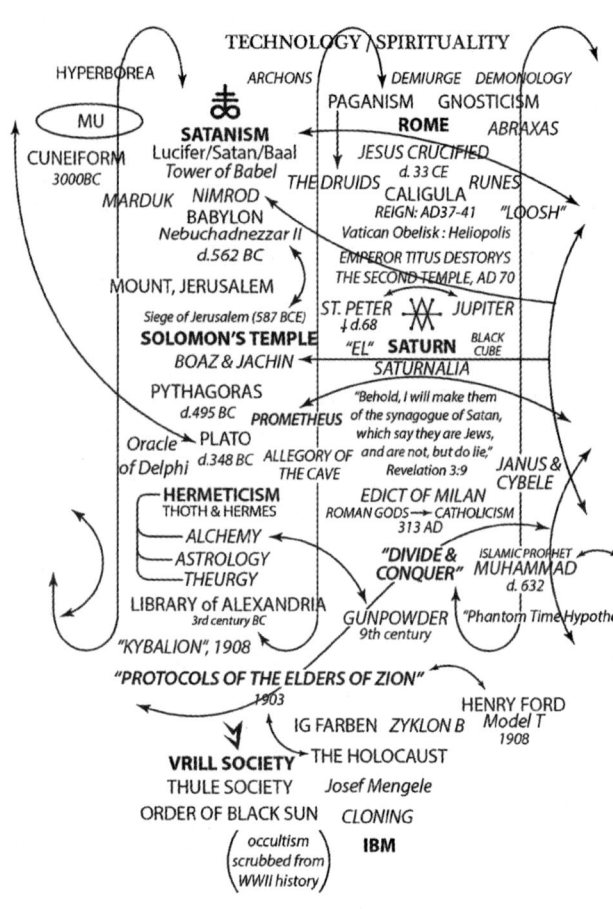

Detail from fig. 1

CONSPIRATORIAL DESIGN

Detail from fig. 1

CONCLUSION

In the premise, I mentioned the metaphorical image of seeing the maze from above. This same image is also presented in a movie by two directors that I consider the most important anti-conspiracy directors: the Coen Brothers. Even though their movies are rarely about conspiracy theories directly, they always deal in some way or another with the human insufficient and often ridicule attempts to bridle chaos. In *The Man Who Wasn't There*[47] the protagonist's ending monologue has a part where he explains how he feels knowing that he is about to die:

> It's like pulling away from the maze. While you're in the maze you go through willy-nilly, turning where you think you have to turn, banging into the dead ends, one thing after another. But get some distance on it, and all those twists and turns, why, they're the shape of your life. It's hard to explain. But seeing it whole gives you some peace.

---

47   *The Man Who Wasn't There*, directed by Coen Brothers, 2001.

The monologue happens during a very lyrical scene. The protagonist is in prison on the night before his execution. After getting involved in a blackmail scheme that went horribly wrong, he was ultimately convicted of a murder he didn't commit. As he says these words he looks into the sky and watches a UFO that sheds a light beam on him and then immediately flies away. Does the UFO mean that he finally understands that aliens were behind the absurd chain of events that led him there? No. It's one last grotesque joke of the Coen brothers, alluding to another character who earlier in the film started believing in UFOs in a phase of denial of grief. Not even right before death the protagonist has some peace from understanding what was going on throughout his whole life. In Coen movies chaos wins, not because everything in their universe is random, or to punish immoral behaviors, but because their characters are never smart enough—they never have enough distance to see it all.

Design discourse has adopted many terms from complex systems theory. It is not uncommon to hear designers speaking of non-linearity, emergence, and feedback loops. But chaos is the property that they always seem to ignore. Accepting that chaos is part of our reality means accepting that some of the patterns that we recognized in the world until a second ago could disappear at any moment. Following the metaphor of the maze, I think that information design shouldn't be an attempt to find the exit of the maze by flying above it, but as annotating the path as we travel through it.

**THE BIGGER PICTURE
CARLO BRAMANTI, 2024**

In 2024, I graduated from Design Academy Eindhoven with a project called *The Bigger Picture*, where I illustrated this same research in an installation consisting of a flowchart game. The diagram was drawn with UV invisible ink directly on the surfaces of the exhibition (walls, floor, columns, and ceiling), resulting in a seemingly empty space. The audience could pick up a UV flashlight to reveal the lines, follow the game, and explore diagram, but only while seeing one small piece of it at a time.

fig. 48 *The Bigger Picture*, image for the Graduation Catalogue 2024 of Design Academy Eindhoven. Photo by Femke Reijerman.

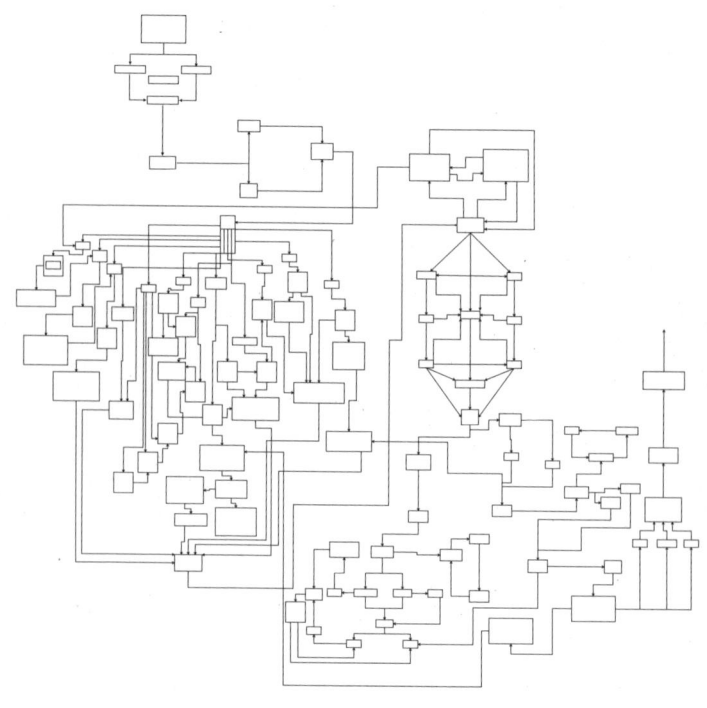

fig. 49 (left) *The Bigger Picture* full flowchart.
(right) Detail from fig. 49

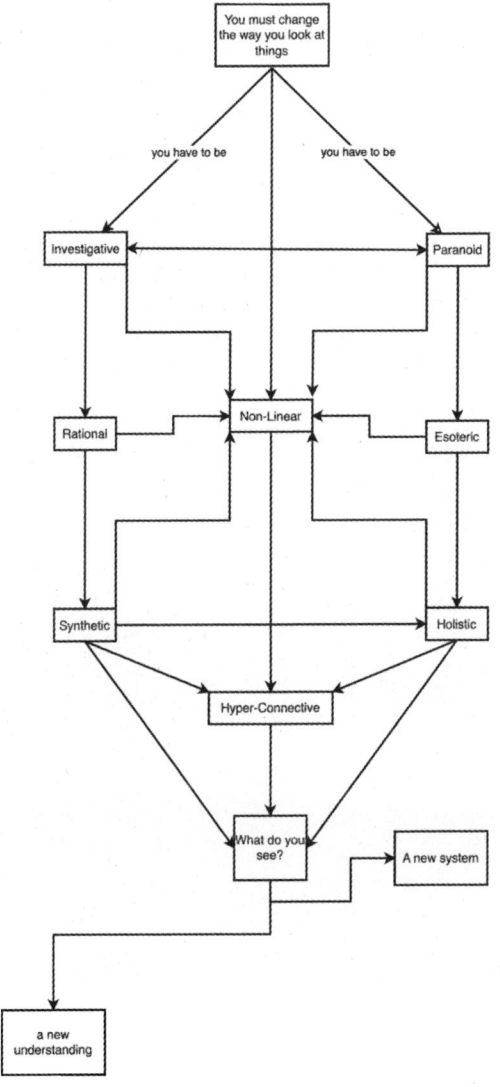

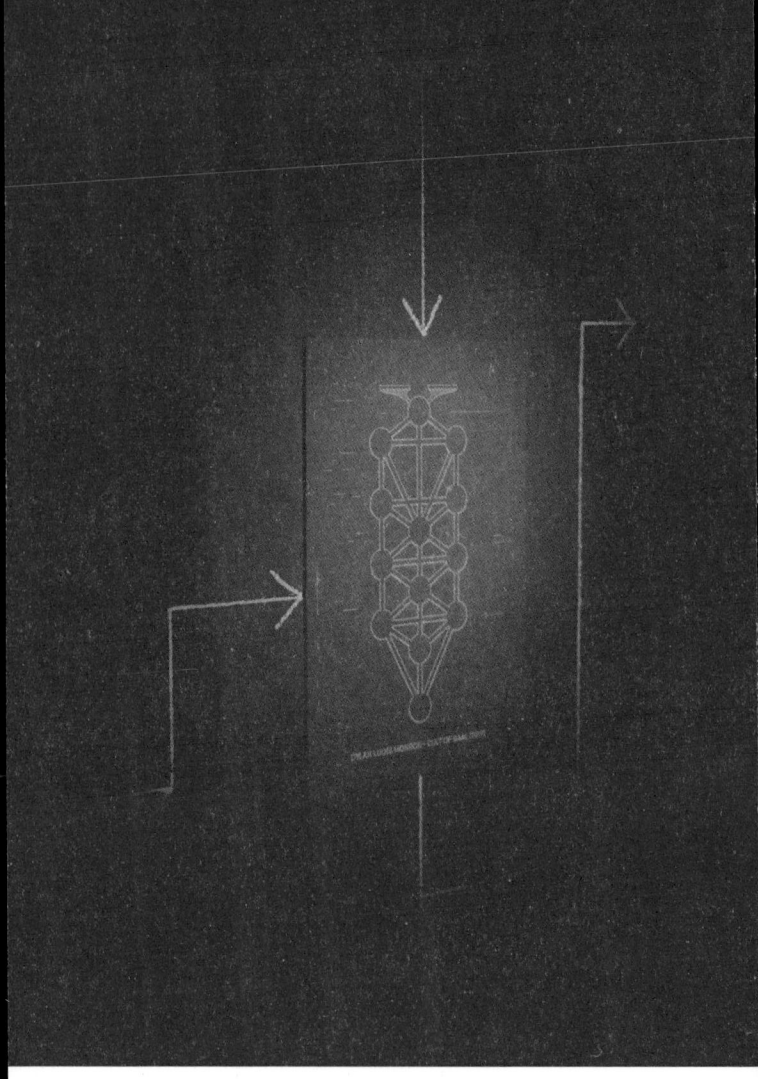

fig. 50-54 *The Bigger Picture* on display on the Graduation Show of Design Academy Eindhoven at the Dutch Design Week 2024. Photos by Sofia Paz, 2024.

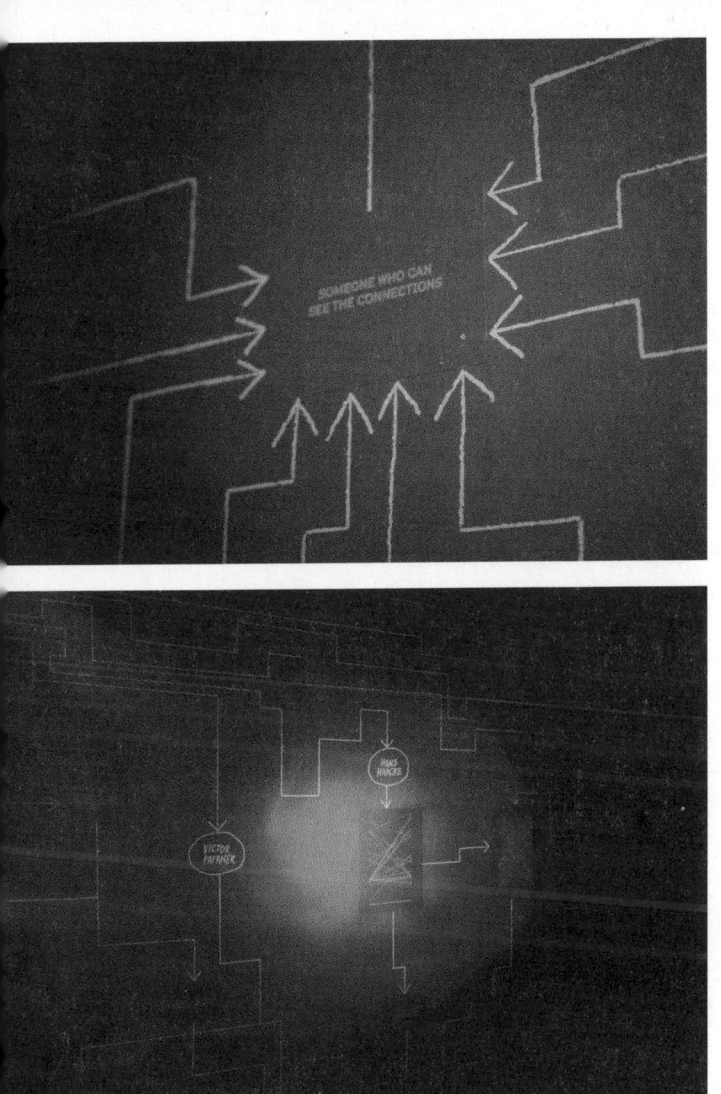

fig. 51 and 52

AFTERWORD
AGAINST COMPLEXITY

SILVIO LORUSSO

"But can one tell if All is a regular crystal, rather
than more probably a monster?"
– Alfred Jarry, 1911

"Information obeys no border. Once deep inside of any single thing
you begin to find connections to everything."
– Don Koberg & Jim Bagnall, 1973

Our world is complex, right? So, how can one speak against something that just *is*? To answer this question, let's consider a very tangible image of complexity (specifically, disorganized complexity), offered by Warren Weaver, a pioneer of communication theory: "a large billiard table with millions of balls rolling over its surface, colliding with one another and with the side rails." This is the level of multiplicity we usually take into account when we speak about complexity (as real-life examples, Weaver mentions a large telephone exchange network and a life insurance company).

Now, I find the image of the billiard table beautiful and straightforward, but also pretty much unusable, unless you are a physicist, a mathematician—or the best pool player in the universe. Very few people work at that level of intricacy, and surely not most designers. Hence, my skepticism toward the idea of complexity as it is currently deployed within design, where every conference, syllabus or project description seems to be about 'complex systems'.

I only became interested in this concept when I started noticing that, not complexity, but the *very talk of complexity* was becoming, in the design field, a cultural practice in its own right. As Guy Julier puts it, "it has become an orthodoxy to talk of the growing complexity of design in our 'complex world'". As with all orthodoxies, one stops questioning the dogmas that sustain them, allowing the primary goal of design—understanding a phenomenon before acting upon it—to be overshadowed by the discipline's own conformism.

Keeping in mind the billiard analogy, one might also argue that the figure best equipped to handle complexity is not the designer, but *the writer*. This is because the writer finds themselves managing a *de facto* complex material, since their arena is the book, an object that appears to be linear and organized only when things are done and only superficially. In truth, the book (like the one you're reading) is a complex object because each word interacts—and does so in multiple ways—with all the others, like and more than Weaver's ivory balls in the pool table.

Furthermore, the idea that the complexity is growing in our society is actually untenable. In a viral (as well as bacterial) article entitled "Design Thinking is Kind of Like Syphilis", Lee Vinsel asks: "What does this claim even mean? Complex in what way? Increasingly complex with respect to what metric? I have asked many professional historians this question, and they believe this increasing complexity claim is unsupportable." Perhaps Theodor Adorno would have agreed, as he once stated that "society, wrongly scolded for its complexity, has in fact become too transparent".

Some time ago, it became evident that many men think about the Roman Empire a lot, like every single day. Personally, I don't, but today I will make an exception and mention a couple of interesting theories about its fall to show that the world has always been shaped by distant, "nonlinear" and obscurely related factors. According to one of these theories, the fall wasn't only due to short-sighted politics or war, but also, significantly, to the lead present in the cups that the members of the Roman elite used to drink, a substance that slowly poisoned them. Marshall McLuhan, on the other hand, building upon the work of Harold Innis, emphasized another factor, namely, a shortage of papyrus, which prevented effective communication on such a vast territory. This is all just to say that a certain degree of interconnectedness is not a unique feature of our present world.

If complexity (in a broad sense) is not a new phenomenon, and complexity (in a narrow sense) is practically useless to us, why is it so present in conversations and articles? The frequency of its use must fulfill another function. To identify it we need to think of how disciplines, and in particular the design discipline, work. Disciplines are arbitrary compartments of knowledge: they strategically define their boundaries in order to isolate some particular problems and solve them, or at least address them. Sociology, for example, was born in the early 19th century to address the problem (and, therefore, problems) of society. However, disciplines won't meekly confine themselves within their artificial boundary; rather, their internal discourse will push the border, extending it. This tendency is especially evident in the design field, where you often hear that "everything is design". Besides the physiological swelling of the disciplines, we witness a phenomenon which is historically specific. Martin Oppenheimer called it a "proletarianization of the professions": when everyone can call themselves a professional, the reputational and financial returns of being one shrink. Furthermore, today there is a tangible distrust toward the figure of the expert. Just think of the field of economy or virology...

AFTERWORD — AGAINST COMPLEXITY

So, what do professionals do to regain prestige? They accelerate the expansion of the disciplinary confines, creating connections in an almost conspiratorial, apophenic mode. This book lucidly captures this process. With his notion of "Conspiratorial Design", Carlo Bramanti shows that there are striking similarities, not only visual but also conceptual, between diagrams by legitimate design figures like Victor Papanek and paranoid-style infographics about "Covid 5G" by an obscure graphic artist named Dylan Louis Monroe. What do these artifacts have in common? They want to produce and project a sense of control on the messiness of the world. After all, as Richard Hofstadter pointed out, "the paranoid mentality is far more coherent than the real world, since it leaves no room for mistakes, failures, or ambiguities". This could also be seen as an excess of the generalizing freedom granted by what Gregory Bateson called "the mysticism of symmetry and pattern". How does the conspiratorial designer project a sense of control? By means of hypertrophy: by adding always more relations to their system, which becomes a totalizing one—it becomes *the* system.

This is why complexity is ultimately a reassuring category. Reassuring to whom? To the professionals, who are there to explain and clarify it, to seal it with "the authoritative stain of scientific enquiry", as Georgina Voss puts it. And there is a further paradox. Do you remember the One Does Not Simply meme derived from Game of Thrones? Well, to reassure themselves, experts will have an incentive to expand their system of reference, and therefore to create more links and relationships. This leads to increasingly big and intricate diagrams, "the airport-bookshop model of systems thinking which tends to involve a lot of graphs and urges to 'shift your mindset'", as Voss again aptly describes it. But by adding links and relationships one does not simply reach "galaxy brain" level. Instead, their insights "can feel like a stoner monologue with pointed hand gestures". Thus, they will likely generate more confusion, more noise, more *chaos*.

Chaos is a mysterious concept, but also one that doesn't require any specific expertise—everyone knows what a chaotic room looks like. Chaos is the professional-disciplinary repressed that returns to haunt the expert of complexity. We hardly find the word 'chaos' in design articles and papers, because chaos is truly scary: it resists organization, it escapes any idea of controllable totality, it leaves us with undecipherable fragments. Whereas complexity reassures us, chaos forces us to confront our own powerlessness.

Shall we then just surrender to it? Not necessarily. As we have seen, complexity as a cultural practice is about totality: *the world* is complex, *society* is complex, etc. However, philosopher Cornelius Castoriadis indicates that the idea of a totality that can be encompassed by the intellect is nothing but a phantom of speculative philosophy. What's more: we do not actually need it in order to exist in the world. Praxis, our acting in the world, is not a plan (closed and exact) but a project (open but not aimless): "every movement is a movement *toward*". And yet, there is something real and concrete about totality. Who, among us, has never felt like the whole world is working against them? This is why, the material upon which praxis acts "does not give itself as totality, [but] it is as totality that evades us."

Praxis is an ongoing negotiation between a general programmatic vision and a partial set of interventions on an "open, self-making unity". While keeping track of its general 'mission', praxis recognizes that it belongs to a given space and time. Seeing its own specific point of view as a feature instead of a bug brings it close to what feminist scholarship calls "situated epistemology". Ultimately, praxis means that we exist within the billiard table, and not outside of it. And as ivory balls must we roll, hoping not to end up in a pocket too soon.

Silvio Lorusso, January 2025

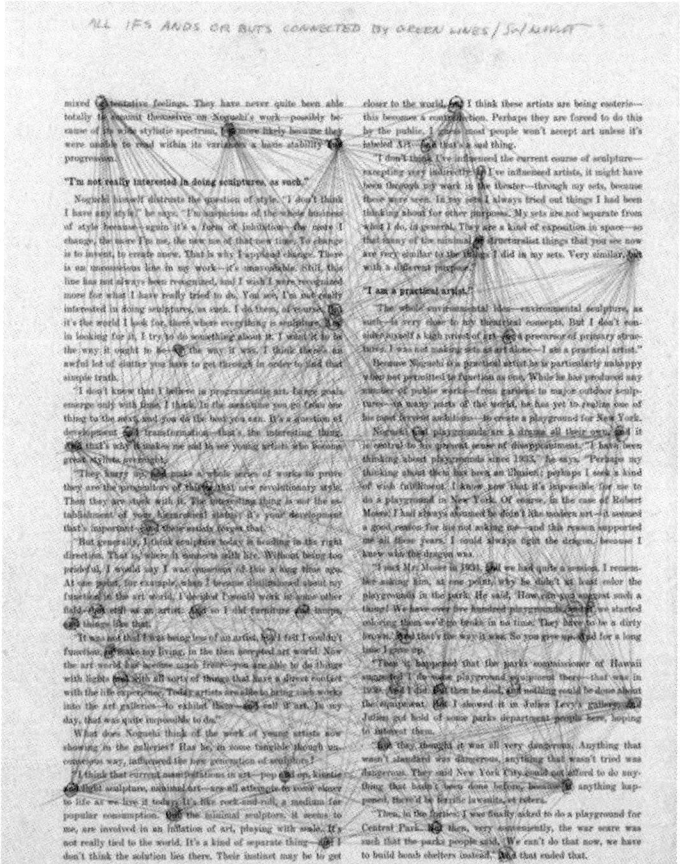

CONSPIRATORIAL DESIGN

fig. 55   *All ifs ands or buts connected by green lines*, Sol LeWitt, 1973.

ACKNOWLEDGEMENTS

At the beginning of this book, I refer to it as a work-in-progress guide, because I believe that all cultural and intellectual work should be open-ended and collaborative, and because I see my work as a give-back to the community of people who think that ideas are a common good. Even if my process was mostly solitary, this book would not exist without the help, support, and care of many people. The first I wish to thank is Silvio Lorusso, who from the beginning saw value in my provocation and contributed immensely to it by always providing me with ideas, enthusiasm, and criticism, and who pushed me to keep working on it after my graduation. Then I want to thank Freek Lomme who believed in the project and advised me preciously. Thanks to Design Academy Eindhoven and particularly the Information Design department where

I developed most of the work: Marco Ferrari (head of department) and the tutors (Geert Staal, Simon Davies, Irene Stracuzzi, Anna Engelhardt, Silvio Lorusso, Tereza Ruller, Vit Ruller, Bram Broerse, Maurits Wouters) as well as all of my classmates (Gioele, Lili, Alice, Claudio, Riko, Miriam, Junn, Ieva, Elias, Adam, and Sofia). Thanks to James Dyer, Tommaso Guariento, Clusterduck, Alessio Pinton and most of all to Sofia Paz for discussing some of the ideas of the book with me and helping me sharpen my ideas and my writing. Thanks to all of my dear friends who, luckily for me, are too numerous and important to name all, but that I always remember. Lastly, a special thanks goes to my family for always being there.

Carlo Bramanti, Rotterdam, 2025

BIBLIOGRAPHY

BOOKS

Angeli, Jacob. *One Mind At A Time: A Deep State of Illusion*. Independently Published, 2020.

Barkun, Michael. *A Culture of Conspiracy: Apocalyptic Visions in Contemporary America*. Berkeley: University of California Press, 2006.

Blauvelt, Andrew. *Hippie Modernism: The Struggle for Utopia*. Minneapolis: Walker Art Center, 2015.

Brinton, Willard Cope. *Graphic Presentation*. Forgotten Books, 2022.

Brotherton, Rob. *Suspicious Minds: Why We Believe Conspiracy Theories*. London: Bloomsbury Sigma, 2016.

Dávila, Patricio. *Diagrams of Power: Visualizing, Mapping, and Performing Resistance*. Eindhoven: Set Margins', 2023.

Drucker, Johanna. *Graphesis: Visual Forms of Knowledge Production*. Massachusetts: Harvard University Press, 2014.

Dunne, Anthony and Raby, Fiona. *Speculative Everything: design, fiction, and social dreaming*. The MIT Press, 2013.

Eco, Umberto. *Foucault's Pendulum*. Translated by William Weaver. New York: Ballantine Books, 1990.

Eco, Umberto. *The Limits of Interpretation: Advances in Semiotics*. Bloomington: Indiana University Press, 1994.

Bureau d'Études. *An Atlas of Agendas: Mapping the Power, Mapping the Commons*. Eindhoven: Set Margins', 2019.

Friedman, Yona. *L'ordre compliqué: et autres fragments*. Paris: Éd. de l'éclat, 2018.

Hofstadter, Richard. *The Paranoid Style in American Politics, and Other Essays*. New York: Vintage Books, 2008.

Jameson, Fredric. *The Geopolitical Aesthetic: Cinema and Space in the World System*. Indianapolis: Indiana University Press British Film Institute, 1995.

Johnson, Herbert F. (Museum of Art). *Mark Lombardi - Global Networks*. Third printing. New York: Independent Curators International, 2004.

Lima, Manuel. *Visual Complexity: Mapping Patterns of Information*. New York: Princeton Architectural Press, 2011.

Lorusso, Silvio. *What Design Can't Do: Essays on Design and Disillusion*. First edition. Eindhoven: Set Margins', 2023.

Magini, Gregorio. *Mitologia del complottismo: il Behemoth delle storie*. First edition. Roma: Tlon, 2024.

Maldonado, Tomás. *La speranza progettuale: ambiente e società*. Edited by Medardo Chiapponi and Raimonda Riccini. Milano: Feltrinelli, 2022.

de Matos, Afonso. *Who Can Afford to Be Critical? An Inquiry into What We Can't Do Alone, as Designers, and into What We Might Be Able to Do Together, as People*. First edition. Eindhoven: Set Margins', 2022.

Otto, Elizabeth. *Haunted Bauhaus: Occult Spirituality, Gender Fluidity, Queer Identities, and Radical Politics*. Cambridge, Massachusetts: The MIT Press, 2019.

Reinfurt, David. *A *new* Program for Graphic Design*. Los Angeles, New York: D.A.P. Distributed Art Publishers, 2019.

Rule, Alix and Levine, David. *International Art English*, Triple Canopy, 2018

Toscano, Alberto and Kinkle, Jeff. *Cartographies of the Absolute*. Winchester: Zero Books, 2015.

Wu Ming 1. *La Q Di Qomplotto: QAnon e Dintorni: Come Le Fantasie Di Complotto Difendono Il Sistema*. Roma: Alegre, 2021.

BIBLIOGRAPHY

ARTICLES

Bishop, Claire. "Information Overload", *Artforum*, September 21, 2023. https://www.artforum.com/features/claire-bishop-on-the-superabundance-of-research-based-art-252571/

Cramer, Florian. "Interview with Florian Cramer | Commentaries: Technology and Policing", *Research Network for Philosophy and Technology*, February 10, 2025. https://philotechne.substack.com/p/interview-with-florian-cramer-commentaries

Groys, Boris. "Self-Design and Aesthetic Responsibility", *e-flux*, June, 2009. https://www.e-flux.com/journal/07/61386/self-design-and-aesthetic-responsibility/

Guariento, Tommaso. "Critica della ragione cospirativa", *Medium*, August 1, 2020. https://tommasoguariento.medium.com/critica-della-ragione-cospirativa-86c38d02c057

Lorusso, Silvio. "*Design Panism: A Timeline*", *Institute of Network Cultures*. March 28, 2021. https://networkcultures.org/entreprecariat/design-panism-a-timeline/

Magini, Gregorio. "L'approccio "comprensivo" al complottismo", *Il Tascabile*. May 14, 2024. https://www.iltascabile.com/linguaggi/approccio-comprensivo-complottismo/

Mattei, Marco "Invito al Reincantamento", *L'Indiscreto*, 2024. https://www.indiscreto.org/invito-al-reincantamento/

Padua, Giovanni. "Serial Experiments Lain e le radici psichiche della cybercultura gnostica", *L'Indiscreto*, 2024. https://www.indiscreto.org/serial-experiments-lain-e-le-radici-psichiche-della-cybercultura-gnostica/

Signorelli, Andrea Daniele. "Il buono delle teorie del complotto", *Il Tascabile*. January 7, 2022. https://www.iltascabile.com/societa/buono-teorie-del-complotto/

Wortham, Jenna. "The Death and Life of Great American GeoCities", *The New York Times Magazine*, February 27, 2015. https://www.nytimes.com/interactive/2015/02/27/magazine/Netstalgia.html

VIDEOS

Pietrusko, Robert. "Dark Optimism: Conspiratorial Styles of Reasoning for the Biosphere", Transmediale, February 2022, Video, 28min. https://youtu.be/ttR2H9klO3M?si=F9A3rx8_F0TRBmDt

Troemel, Brad. "Art School Report", Patreon, October 2024, Video, 40min. https://www.patreon.com/posts/art-school-113925321

Troemel, Brad. "The KAYFABE Report", Patreon, August 2022, Video, 54min. https://www.patreon.com/posts/kayfabe-report-70281334

Wu Ming, "Come nasce una teoria del complotto: il caso QAnon - di Wu Ming 1", YouTube, April 2019, Video, 61min. https://www.youtube.com/watch?v=76yMhwUfoys&t=1101s&ab_channel=WuMing

FILMS

Carpenter, John, director. *They Live*. Universal Pictures, 1988. 94 min.

Coen, Joel & Ethan, director. *The Man Who Wasn't There*. USA Films, 2001. 116 min.

Coppola, Francis Ford, director. *Megalopolis*. Lionsgate Films, 2024. 138 min.

BIBLIOGRAPHY

SOURCE OF THE IMAGES

fig.1	https://dsmp.io/product/q-key-poster-white-24-x-36-2025-edition/
fig.2-9	https://www.reddit.com/r/conspiracy/
fig.10	Source unknown
fig.11	https://sitcomtheory.org/ABSTRACTION
fig.12	https://dsmp.io/product/healing-web-poster-24-x-36%e2%80%b3-us/
fig.13	https://superpredator.zone/
fig.14	https://socks-studio.com/2012/08/22/mark-lombardi/
fig.15	Bureau d'Études. *An Atlas of Agendas: Mapping the Power, Mapping the Commons*. Eindhoven: Set Margins', 2019.
fig.16	Courtesy of the author
fig.17	https://www.reddit.com/r/conspiracy/comments/4gke31/meet_artist_mark_lombardi_he_created_maps_of_the/
fig.18	Jones, John Christopher. *Design Methods*. New York, Wiley, 1992.
fig.19	https://en.m.wikipedia.org/wiki/File:Kircher_Tree_of_Life.png
fig.20	https://deepstatemappingproject.com/product/cult-of-baal-pfd-download/
fig.21	https://socks-studio.com/2016/05/02/the-knowledge-box-by-ken-isaacs-1962/
fig.22	https://en.wikipedia.org/wiki/Flammarion_engraving#/media/File:Flammarion.jpg
fig.23	https://www.macba.cat/en/obra/r3623-dow-shalt-not-kill-usa---union-of-stoned-anarchists/
fig.24	https://sheldonartmuseum.org/work/untitled-i-gerald-ford-am-the-38th-puppet-of-the-united-states/
fig.25	https://www.designatlarge.it/libri-che-ogni-designer-dovrebbe-leggere/
fig.26	Blauvelt, Andrew. *Hippie Modernism: The Struggle for Utopia*. Minneapolis: Walker Art Center, 2015.
fig.27	https://www.mdpi.com/2071-1050/7/8/9864
fig.28	https://archive.org/details/chepfl-lipr-AXC34_01/page/n195/mode/2up
fig.29	https://garadinervi-repertori.blog/post/675746654984519680/hans-haacke-shapolsky-et-al-manhattan-real
fig.30	Courtesy of the author
fig.31	https://www.instagram.com/reel/DJ6aUknomZc/
fig.32	https://dismagazine.com/distaste/73360/metahaven-sunshine-unfinished/
fig.33	https://calculatingempires.net/
fig.34	https://www.flickr.com/photos/densitydesign/3975416561/in/album-72157622379836675/
fig.35	https://cloudcosmogram.space/index.html
fig.36	https://en.wikipedia.org/wiki/File:Snow-cholera-map-1.jpg
fig.37	https://monoskop.org/File:Gropius_Walter_Idee_und_Aufbau_des_staatlichen_bauhauses_Weimar_1923.pdf
fig.38	https://link.springer.com/article/10.1007/s00146-021-01339-1

fig.39 https://oxman.com/mission
fig.40 https://medium.com/@pricharielp/design-for-inclusion-social-justice-and-sustainability-dissecting-the-legacy-and-creative-7725ac70ab90
fig.41 https://x.com/graphific/status/1078428787363270659
fig.42 https://commons.wikimedia.org/wiki/File:Ramon_Llull_-_Ars_Magna_Fig_1.png
fig.43 https://www.francescofranchi.com/memory-palace
fig.44 https://archive.org/details/the-universal-one-1926-walter-russell
fig.45 https://x.com/carpethefish/status/1752621448680845540
fig.46 Jones, John Christopher. *Design Methods*. New York, Wiley, 1992.
fig.47 https://www.instagram.com/p/C4n9Fz3shCd/?img_index=1
fig.48 Original image
fig.49 Original image
fig.50-54 Courtesy of the author
fig.55 https://www.vaultofculture.com/vault/nst/2024/07/09/soldewitt